# DEALING WITH DIFFICULT TEACHERS

## SECOND EDITION

### Todd Whitaker

EYE ON EDUCATION
6 Depot Way West, Suite 106
Larchmont, N.Y.  10538

**Library of Congress Cataloging-in-Publication Data**

Whitaker, Todd, 1959-
    Dealing with difficult teachers / Todd Whitaker.--2nd ed.
        p.   cm.
    Includes bibliographical references
    ISBN  1-930556-45-4
    1. Teacher effectiveness--United States.   2. Teacher-principal relationships--United States.   3. Teachers--Dismissal of--United States.   4. School personnel management--United States.   I. Title.

LB2832.2.W516   2002
371.4'4--dc21                                    2002075235

Production services provided by:
ComManagement
1211 Courtland Drive
Raleigh, NC 27604
919.833.3350

# About the Author

**Dr. Todd Whitaker** is a Professor of Educational Leadership at Indiana State University in Terre Haute, Indiana. Prior to coming to Indiana, he was a middle and high school principal in Missouri. In addition, Dr. Whitaker served as middle school coordinator in Jefferson City, Missouri, where he supervised the development of two new middle schools.

Dr. Whitaker has been published in the areas of principal effectiveness, teacher leadership, change, staff motivation, instructional improvement, and middle-level practices. His books include *What Great Principals Do Differently: 15 Things That Matter Most*, *Motivating & Inspiring Teachers*, *Dealing with Difficult Parents (and with Parents in Difficult Situations)*, *Teaching Matters: Motivating and Inspiring Yourself*, and *Feeling Great! The Educator's Guide for Eating Better, Exercising Smarter, and Feeling Your Best*.

He is a highly sought presenter and has made hundreds of state, national, and international presentations. Todd is married to Beth who is a former principal and currently is Associate Professor of Elementary Education at Indiana State. They have served as co-editors of *Contemporary Education*, an international journal. They have three children: Katherine, Madeline, and Harrison.

# Preface

My interest in writing this book is the result of three different occurrences in my educational career. The first happened during my first year of teaching. Like most educators, I chose the field because of the chance to have a positive impact on the lives of young people. I started my career in a rural K–12 school, where I taught business education, mathematics, and where I served as coach. I felt that I was a fine teacher, and I was working to have a positive impact on the students and community. However, just down the hall was a teacher who yelled, humiliated students, and was sarcastic with her students on a regular basis. I thought if I could do something about her treatment of students, then that improvement could be more valuable than anything I might accomplish in my own classroom. Thus, I became a principal.

The second experience came when I became the assistant principal, then principal, of a school that employed some marginal (a kind word) staff members. Many of these teachers had been in education, and in this school, for a number of years. Actually, I was ashamed to have students go into the classrooms of some of the faculty. In addition, whenever we attempted to improve our school, we had faculty who chimed in with statements such as, "It didn't work back in '36; it won't work now!" Unfortunately many staff followed their lead. I knew that for our school to be outstanding, something had to be done to make the teaching staff more effective *and* at the same time develop a culture and climate in the school that supported positive change among all staff.

The third factor, which supports the approaches that follow, was that I was fortunate to have an outstanding assistant principal in one of the schools where I was principal. In addition to low staff morale in the school there were several difficult teachers in the building. Together, my assistant principal and I implemented many of the approaches that are described in this book. We were fortunate to have success in altering the climate of the school. We were also able to generate some needed turnover with some of our most difficult and negative teachers. Then, as often happens with great assistant principals, he was given his own school. His school was in need of effective leadership and had several difficult staff members. As a new principal in a challenging setting, he was able to implement some of the same concepts we had developed together. This parallel success led to the further development of these approaches, which are non-confrontational in style and can be implemented in any school immediately. Since the time of those experiences, having worked with numerous schools, I have been able to verify that the approaches that worked in my schools work in all schools.

This book is designed to be a practitioner-oriented resource that principals can use to improve their school by helping them to work effectively with their most difficult teachers.

Todd Whitaker, Ph.D.
Professor
Indiana State University
Terre Haute

# Introduction to the First Edition

I have written this book for a very simple reason: Education is the single most important profession that there is. No other profession has the same impact on the future of society than one in education. This love for children and for schools was my driving force behind *Dealing with Difficult Teachers*.

It is important for the reader to understand that I do not know of any school administrator anywhere who values teachers more than I do. I know that the key to a great school is an outstanding teaching staff. However, there is one group of individuals that I value even more than teachers—the students. The students are the reason for which I am writing this book. It is crucial to me that every student be treated in an appropriate, caring manner each day at school. For many students, school is the highlight of their day and the educators they come in contact with are the primary determinants of what kind of a day each day will be. Great educators can make students' days great; negative and ineffective educators can demoralize students and colleagues. Difficult teachers can ruin the day.

Another important element in dealing with difficult teachers is the belief that adults determine how they are going to behave and interact with others every day. Students may not have the level of maturity to be as responsible as adults for their behavior and for some of the choices that they make. Because education is so important, however, it is critical that each adult who comes in contact with students have a positive and productive manner of treating them.

One of our great challenges as principals is moving past the assumption that everyone is in the field of education for the same reason we are—to do what is best for the children in our school. We should always be open to that hope and expectation, but for whatever reason, we may find ourselves facing people whose current behavior is not in the best interest of the students. One of the most challenging tasks principals face in dealing with difficult teachers is moving out of the natural nurturing role. Principals are caring people in a profession that requires this approach. If, in our organization, we have other adults who choose not to behave with the best interests of children in mind, then we have to make every effort to alter the behaviors of the staff members or remove them from working with students.

This book is not designed to be a first step. It was developed to assist the principal when all previous attempts have not been successful. It is geared toward our most challenging faculty. The practices included are not designed for the new teacher who is struggling a little with classroom management nor are the practices intended for the teacher who is pretty effective, but whom you wish would be a little more innovative. Although some of these concepts will apply, this book is designed for the most frustrating, resistant, ineffective, and negative staff in the school. Remember, nobody likes to deal with these individuals, but the good principals do and do so effectively. It is also critical for the principal to keep an open mind regarding improvement versus perfection. As embarrassing as it is to admit, if most difficult teachers would only try a little bit more or improve just a fair amount, they would make a big difference in the school. They do not have to become the best teachers in order for the school to improve. They just need to discontinue being the worst. This is not where we eventually want to be, but it is important to be aware continually that any positive growth is movement in the right direction.

This book is not about the formal evaluation process. As principals are well aware, the evaluation process is only part of improving staff performance. Moreover, the formal evaluation process is often limited in effectiveness by the forms, paperwork, and even contractual guidelines. There are several other resources available to assist with this facet of leadership. Instead, this work applies to all 180 days of the school year in ways that are much less cumbersome and limiting in nature.

No strategy in this book is easy. We have solved the easy problems. Effectively leading people is never easy. This is particularly true with our most difficult staff. There is not a principal around who wants to deal with the most challenging staff members. No one looks forward to it.

We can resolve glitches in our schedule. Determining the most efficient way to operate the lunch lines can eventually be achieved in every school. However, any time you are dealing with people, it is never easy. Many approaches in this book are simple to understand, but they take much resolve on the part of the building principal to apply. Dealing with difficult teachers is never easy. Doing what is best for kids is often not easy either. Great principals somehow find a way to do both.

# Introduction to the Second Edition

It is exciting to be writing a second edition of this book. The reaction to the first edition has been remarkable and overwhelming. Interestingly, I chose *Dealing with Difficult Teachers* as my first book for two reasons. One of them was that there seemed to be few resources on the topic itself. There are books on evaluation, but that is not the same issue. We cannot wait for a negative staff member's three-year evaluation of difficult teachers for them to change. It is essential that they improve their behavior more quickly. Additionally, if the principal is documenting a teacher's poor performance, then the principal is working. Instead, it is important that the difficult teacher be the one doing the work.

The lack of information regarding improving challenging staff members is surprising because the problem is so common. Almost every school has teachers who work against school improvement and do not have students as their central focus. Yet evidence in achieving change in the behavior of the troubled teachers is not very evident. When a principal can successfully work with the most difficult staff members and concurrently increase his or her own credibility with the rest of the staff members, then the principal has probably solved the most challenging task a building administrator can face. If a school leader can master this one, then the rest should be simple.

The other reaction that has been so positive is from teachers—not the difficult ones, but from all of their peers. Good teachers are just as troubled and ashamed of their difficult colleagues as principals are. And they have not had a resource to utilize either. I have received tremendous positive feedback from teachers who have found the book beneficial. Because we avoid power struggles in our solutions, the majority of the approaches are applicable to working with peers and even difficult supervisors!

Principals have discovered the positive result of sharing the book with staff members instead of hiding the book in a desk drawer. After all, many of our teachers have worked with these troubled teachers much longer than we have.

The second edition specifically addresses some of the issues that educators most frequently raise when they come to one of my workshops on this topic. The new four-chapter section (Part 4) focuses on communicating with the difficult teacher. Specific issues include strategies that work most effectively when addressing and communicating with difficult teachers regarding their behavior. In other words, when should I approach the teacher? Is the timing a factor in attempting to change negative behavior? Are there more effective questioning strategies? We also discuss additional methods to ensure that we are gaining credibility with the many positive and productive teachers in our school. These key teachers will ultimately determine just how far our school will go.

I appreciate all the kind words and feedback that you have shared regarding the effectiveness of the strategies in *Dealing with Difficult Teachers*. I am glad that you have found them to be beneficial in your schools. After speaking to a group of educators recently, a teacher passed me a note that she carries with her. The note said, "An incompetent teacher is much worse than an incompetent surgeon, because an incompetent surgeon only cuts up one person at a time." The hurt that a poor teacher can inflict on our students is immeasurable. It is up to the principal to have a positive impact on the situation. When you make a difference in your school you make a difference in children's lives. I want to personally thank you for your dedication to making your schools a better place for the teachers and for the students.

# Table of Contents

# Part 1

# The Principal and the Difficult Teacher

# 1

# What Is a Difficult Teacher?

Think of the most difficult teachers you know. What do you think of? In other words, what adjectives would you use to describe them? What characteristics come to mind? In asking many groups of principals, superintendents, teachers, and students this question, several words and phrases keep coming up. Terms and phrases that are frequently used to describe these difficult teachers include:

- lazy
- negative
- resistant to change
- boring
- negative leader
- belligerent
- inflexible
- back stabber
- domineering
- stubborn
- don't like kids
- don't like their job
- don't like themselves
- counting the days until they retire
- counting the days until school ends (and it is early October!)
- rude
- cannot get along with others
- lectures
- argumentative
- cynical

Not a real glamorous list is it?

Now ask yourself, "What is it that these people would be good at?" You do not see many of these terms on a job description, do you? The answer, of course, is that they would not be good at anything. That is why they do not quit education! There is nothing else they can do effectively either. What employer wants a lazy, negative, rude, back stabber? That is why your most challenging staff members seemingly stay in your building forever. Believe me, they are well aware of the fact that they could not be successful at any of life's employment options.

However, before you give up hope, take another look at the list of characteristics. Does anything else come to mind? The adjectives on the list are personal traits. They all can be used to describe the personalities of negative people. If they are personal traits, however, perhaps these difficult individuals have a choice to be this way or not. It is up to them. Each one of us decides how many arguments we get in each year; each one of us chooses to be negative or positive. We all decide whether to be cynical, back-stabbing, or lazy. It is truly a personal decision. While this may sound hopeless for the people in your school, it really is a reason for optimism. Because each of these are traits that your difficult teachers *choose* to express, they may also be things they could choose *not* to express.

This implies that as an educational leader, you have the possibility of transforming the most challenging faculty. However, no one ever said it would be easy. Let us take a look at these most difficult teachers in a different context. In a school context, what makes a teacher challenging? There are at least six general areas that may cause you to label teachers difficult. These include:

**Classroom Behavior.** Obviously one of the first determinants of whether someone is a difficult teacher is learning what these teachers are doing in the classroom. Are they effective in working with students on a daily basis? If the answer is no, then you must work to motivate these teachers to take a different approach in their classes.

Sometimes we feel that if a person is going to retire in three years, we can just let them go until then. This may be true in other professions. If you were the manager of a company, you could "hide" an employee for a period of time. Maybe you could reduce workload or limit contact with the customers. In education, however, the standard is much higher for one simple reason: They come in daily contact with children. Teachers' jobs are so important that we cannot afford to allow ineffective teachers to continue carte blanche. Being an educator is too significant an occupation to allow ineffective people to remain in the profession.

It is difficult for a principal to sleep at night if even one child in school walks through that difficult teacher's door each day. Even more unfortunately, there are few situations that involve only one child. Instead, negative teachers typically affect 25 to 150 students each school day. The standard of acceptable performance in education is higher simply because it is education. One thing to remember is this: If a teacher has approached students ineffectively for 28 consecutive years, he or she has been *allowed* to do so by principals for 28 consecutive years. This implies that if you are the principal you must cause ineffective teachers to change their behaviors.

Students are often willing to share feelings they have about their teachers. A principal who is accessible, visible, and a good listener can often validate observations through dialogues. Conversations with students can provide additional perspectives regarding teacher effectiveness.

There is a simple test to determine whether your teachers fit into the standard of difficult classroom teacher. You need to ask yourself whether you would want your own son or daughter in their classes. If the answer is "no," then it should be difficult to have a clear conscience in scheduling any students into these teachers' classrooms. The simple technique of making the measurement personal by involving your own children is a good determinant of a difficult teacher.

How teachers and all educators treat the young people they come in contact with every day is a non-negotiable measure of their effectiveness. Altering this behavior, which often has been in place for many years, can be a challenging task for the school leader.

**Staff Influence.** There is nothing more damaging to a school, especially one attempting to bring about positive change, than a negative teacher-leader. A negative teacher-leader is someone who cannot only fight good ideas, but—worse yet—one who can convince other teachers to be negative as well. Sometimes these teachers are not particularly poor classroom teachers. They often have some level of interpersonal skills. These interpersonal strengths often increase their level of influence. However, you must reduce the negative influence of these people, or it becomes very difficult to implement new programs or ideas. Many times if you can reduce their negative influence, then you can tolerate them in the classroom.

The challenge of reducing their influence without losing credibility with the remainder of the faculty is essential. Diminishing the relationship between the principal and this negative teacher-leader might diminish the relationship between the principal and some of the staff members who look to this negative leader for guidance. Do not allow this possibility to be a rationale for inaction. For a school to move forward in an effective direction, it is essential that the productive, positive staff members provide the momentum and direction for the school and staff. Reducing the ability of the most negative and resistant staff to cause other staff members to "drag their feet" is a critical part of this process.

**Public Perception.** Everyone wants to associate with a winner. To determine whether this is true, we need only look at our local college basketball team. If the team has success, there is a much greater likelihood it has fan support, money donations, and good basketball recruits attending the school. If a team is struggling, even though it needs support more than the successful team, people tend to distance themselves from the program. In a way, the same holds true for schools. If people perceive a school as successful, parents are more likely to get involved with the school. Local businesses are much more willing to associate with the school. Thus, it is essential that there be a positive public perception of schools and teachers.

The perception of a school is often a combination of the perceptions of all of the individuals in the organization. If we have individuals who are viewed negatively by parents, central office, or the community, can have a draining effect on the entire school.

If you have staff members who continually do things that offend or incite others outside the school, it is very harmful to the credibility of the principal and of the school as a whole. Additionally, a staff member who frequently upsets others causes an increased burden on the already demanding load of the principal. Having to "mop up" after these individuals is very stressful and time-consuming. It should not occur.

As a principal, the majority of parent concerns and phone calls pertain to one or two staff members. Year after year parental complaints revolve around a few teachers. If parents call these staff members prior to calling you, the parents' interactions with these difficult teachers will just make bad situations worse.

Think about preparing for the annual start-of-the-year open house or for an upcoming parent-teacher conference. Do you have staff members who will leave such negative impressions with mothers and fathers that you can anticipate calls from and meetings with parents? Many parents will request (demand) that their children be reassigned. And to be truthful, you cannot even blame the parent for desiring this. You would like to take all students out of their classes. These difficult teachers create a public perception that is very negative and harmful to the school.

Consider the impact of a negative teacher who is in line at the grocery store on a Friday afternoon on the way home from work. In the line next to this teacher is your PTA president—a very nice, friendly, and supportive parent. The parent says to the teacher sincerely, "Have a nice weekend!" The difficult teacher is the one who responds in a sarcastic tone, "Yeah, maybe I can, since I don't have to deal with those kids for two days!" This contact establishes such a negative tone and feeling for the school. We have to help alter the behavior of the teacher in order to continue to build the credibility and reputation of our school.

**Resistance to Change.** Have you and several faculty experienced growing enthusiasm for a new program? Just as that enthusiasm balloon was filling with energy, was there a staff member waiting to pull out a pin and pop it?

Nearly everyone resists change; that is natural. This reluctance is a normal reaction to the fear of the unknown. However, some individuals go far beyond this normal apprehensiveness. They fight, attack, and attempt to sabotage improvement attempts. Their efforts regularly thwart any type of change. This is often true even though the change does not affect them. They just see their role as protecting the status quo.

Many times a principal must develop an understanding of their methods of resistance and the informal dynamics they have that affect so many others in the school. This understanding can be an important factor in working with the most difficult faculty.

**Dampen Enthusiasm/Damage Climate.**   Good staff morale and school climate are essential to a productive and successful school. Teachers who constantly drain excitement, enthusiasm, climate, and culture must be contained. These difficult teachers cannot continue to be such a burden on the positive staff members in the school. In order for schools to be as effective as they need to be in working with our students, principals have to alter the behavior and minimize the effect that these negative teachers have on other staff members.

Individuals who consistently complain in the teachers' workroom or lounge can often have a substantial crippling effect on an entire school. What is the most reliable predictor of whether teachers will be griping in the teachers' lounge tomorrow? Most likely it is whether they were griping in the teachers' lounge today. The faculty who make negative comments or continually complain at staff meetings can set the tone for the entire school, if they continue. It is critical that the principal be aware of the result of these inappropriate behaviors and reduce both the behaviors and their potential impact. Often behaviors like these become habits and we have to effectively intervene in order to change this environment in a productive manner.

**Parade of Students to the Office.**   If someone had asked you last July to predict the three teachers in your school who would send the highest number of students to the office in the upcoming school year, could you have done it? Can you predict which teachers will refer the most students to the office for discipline next year? You probably can. Even more amazingly, you do not even have to know beforehand which students are going to be enrolled in their classes! We know that the behavior of the teachers is generally more of a determinant of office referrals than the students' behavior. That is why we can usually predict how many students will be sent to the office from each classroom. Selfishly, as well as educationally, principals need to get these inappropriate teacher behaviors to change. Otherwise we can never get out of the reactive mode. The truly difficult teachers generally have the "messiest" discipline situations to sort out. This is often true because their methods are difficult to defend and yet the teachers still need to be supported.

Principals often cite time as their biggest need in order to increase their effectiveness as instructional leaders. Many times, especially in schools with no assistant principals, the building leader spends a disproportionate amount of time reacting to problems sent by difficult teachers. I have often thought of it as the 10/90 rule. Ten percent of our teachers generate 90 percent of the discipline referrals in a school. A building leader who could get these difficult teachers to alter their behavior in the classroom, or at least stop parading students to the office, could put much more time and energy into being a proactive leader. Stopping this long line of office referrals from just a few staff members without being viewed as unsupportive of teachers is essential for effective instructional leadership.

The approaches that follow in this book are applicable to each of these types of difficult teachers. Many of the concepts are applicable to a variety of the different, troubling staff members.

# 2

# Three Kinds of Teachers

In order to have a positive effect on altering the inappropriate behaviors of the most difficult staff members, it is imperative to develop an understanding of some of the dynamics that are taking place in your school. It is also crucial to establish some common terminology, which will be used frequently in the upcoming chapters.

A perspective on understanding the different types of teachers is offered by Dr. Al Burr (1993), a former high school principal in the St. Louis area. He believes that there are three kinds of teachers in a school: *superstars*, *backbones*, and *mediocres*.

Burr explains that the way to determine the category of each teacher is fairly simple. *Superstars* are rare; they constitute the top 3 to 10 percent of teachers in a school. Many schools may have only one or two people who fall into this category. A few outstanding schools may have 8 to 10. They are often the students' favorite teachers. Parents regularly request that their children be placed in the superstars' classrooms. A final, but critical, litmus test of superstars is that they are *respected* by all or almost all other faculty members. This is an important measure. It implies that a superstar cannot be perceived as the "principal's pet," because of the respect factor. They can *be* the favorite teacher of the building administrator, but they cannot be *perceived* in that fashion or else they may lose the respect of the other staff members. A quick definition: A superstar is a teacher who, if he or she left your faculty, could probably not be replaced with another teacher who is as good or effective as the departing educator. Burr also adds that superstars want two things: autonomy and recognition. This is important to remember as we think about working with our most challenging staff.

The second category of teachers are the *backbones*. Backbones are good, solid teachers—the heart of the faculty. They traditionally constitute 80 to 90 percent of your staff. They are good, stable, hard-working teachers. A quick determination of which teachers are backbones is that if two or three of your backbone teachers left your staff, you could probably do about as well in replacing them. You would consistently want to hire the rare superstar, but on a routine basis when a backbone quit, you could hire someone who is nearly as effective. This is not an indictment of backbones; it is just a way to develop an understanding of their impact on the faculty dynamics.

Casey Stengel, the legendary baseball manager, described leading a baseball team in this fashion: A manager has 5 players who love him, 5 players who hate him, and 15 players sitting on the fence. The key to being a good manager is to keep the 15 who are sitting on the fence from moving over to the side of the 5 who hate him.

Leading a school effectively may better be described as the process of getting the 15 backbones onto the side with the superstars. Dwight Eisenhower described leadership in this way: "Leadership is the art of getting other people to do something you want done because they want to do it." Figuring out the most effective way to continue to enhance and develop the skills of the majority of your staff, the backbones, is an essential part of the role of an effective principal.

The third category, the *mediocres*—which may be too kind a word—are identifiable by some of the terms we described in Chapter 1. There is another way to establish which of the teachers in your school are mediocres. Think through your faculty. Ask yourself, "For which of these people could I easily find a more effective replacement?" Which teachers' resignations or transfers would please you? Which teachers' absences wou[ld] benefit the school? Those teachers who come to mind are likely to be mediocres. Although mediocres are the teachers that we most often identify as difficult staff, some characteristics of difficult people may at times fit backbones as well. In other words, some teachers may be adequate in the classroom (backbone), but have other negative characteristics they bring to the school. However, the majority of the difficult teachers we will discuss in the book are likely to fit into the category of mediocres. Generally mediocre teachers are ineffective in the classroom. Additionally, they can provide other challenges that compound the burden they place on a school and its leader.

Peers may not always be aware of the effectiveness of other staff members. Thus, the informal leadership of a school may come from teachers who fall into each of these categories. Additionally, formal leadership roles such as department chair, team leader, or grade level leader may be in the hands of teachers with varying classroom capabilities.

A principal must be aware that each type of teachers presents differing needs and challenges. Being aware of the resulting dynamics is important in helping a school to become more effective.

## Autonomy of the Superstar—An Important Ingredient to Success

It is valuable to understand the application of autonomy to superstars. This autonomy implies that we should not try to control the behavior of our less effective staff by rules. The reason is this: Every time we put in a rule we are doing it to try to alter the behavior of our more negative influences. The problem with new rules is that the superstars are most likely to follow it. Thus, they will lose some autonomy. We must look for other means of working with our mediocres and other difficult staff members.

When deciding to implement a new policy or "rule," there is a quick three-question quiz you can ask yourself to determine whether this policy is likely to have a positive or negative effect. These three questions are:

*true* purpose in implementing this rule

ly accomplish this purpose?
ˈ most positive and productive people
ˌ policy?

This sounds very basic—and it is. However, it can be a powerful measure regarding not only future implementations, but it can also help determine the value of current procedures. Let us apply these questions to a scenario that is very common in many schools. On many school doors the first thing that greets parents, guests, and others is a sign in bold type:

**ALL VISITORS MUST REPORT TO THE OFFICE!**

Using the three questions posed earlier, we can determine the impact this procedure has.

1. *What is my true purpose in implementing this rule or policy?* Our instinctual reaction in answering this question may be, "So that all visitors go to the office and sign in so that we can be aware of who is in the building." No doubt that this could be one reason. However, the underlying reason is to prevent someone from entering our school secretly and harming or abducting a student. This is a valiant aim, yet is this likely to be the result? Which leads us to:

2. *Will it actually accomplish this purpose?* The obvious answer to this question is, "no." Someone who is attempting to do harm to a student or faculty member is not going to be dissuaded by a sign on the front door. If they bring a weapon into the school they are unlikely to "check their gun at the office," so to speak. In actuality, this sign is unlikely to accomplish the positive purpose that motivated its placement. In situations where the answer to question number two is "yes" or even "maybe," this does not mean that this new idea should be implemented. Regardless of the potential result on our difficult visitors (or staff members), we need to weigh this potentially positive effect against any harm that may result to our positive people. So this brings us to the third question:

*3. How will my most positive and productive people feel about this policy?* When a sign on the front door of a store says in bold print "All Shoplifters Will Be Prosecuted!" does this make you feel warm and welcome in the store? Do you think that this actually prevents someone who is planning on breaking the law from stealing? Obviously not. What the store owner has chosen to do with this sign is make the customers uncomfortable with a sign that will most likely be ignored or laughed at by the people at whom it is directed.

This same effect is likely to occur in our schools. Ordering someone to do something is never a positive approach. Additionally, it is a reminder to every supportive parent who enters the school that something bad could happen to children when they are at school. You have chosen to place the feelings of our positive and supportive people below the hopeful effect of a rule that will not work anyway.

As building leaders, we often verbalize that we wish more parents and community members would become involved in schools. By our actions, we may be sending another more negative message. Realizing that this sign has no effect on intruders and has a negative effect on the vast majority of people who enter our school each day (including setting a negative smart-aleck tone for the students), we should reexamine this procedure. You could accomplish the desired result to the same degree by keeping our positive supporters in mind:

**Welcome parents and visitors! We are glad you are here. We do ask that all parents, visitors, and guests sign in at the office. Thank you for visiting Smith Middle School.**

The final support you need to offer is directions to the office. After all, a visitor probably does not know how to get there. With this scenario in mind, you can apply these same three questions to rules and procedures we attempt to implement in order to control our difficult staff members and determine whether they are likely to have an appropriate and positive effect on our school.

A couple of common scenarios that arise in schools are faculty using the copier too much or using supplies (folders, Post-It™ notes, paper, etc.) at a frequency that will exceed the budget. Our instinct is that there are most likely a few people who are using things in an inappropriate manner or maybe even using some of these items for personal uses. You are tempted to implement much tighter restrictions on using the copier or accessing supplies. You may require that all staff sign a piece of paper indicating how many copies they make. Or you might have all staff sign a list when they take supplies. You may even issue a memo, directing staff to reduce their use of the copier or supplies—kind of a guilty-until-proven-innocent approach. You can apply our three rules and determine whether this approach is appropriate.

1. *What is my true purpose in implementing this rule or policy?* The purpose in putting forth this rule is to prevent those people who are wastefully using the copier or taking too many supplies from continuing these practices.

2. *Will it actually accomplish this purpose?* If someone is doing something inappropriate, the person most likely knows it is inappropriate and just chooses to do it anyway. No one assumes that it is *acceptable* to run copies of Christmas card letters on the school copier. Some people, however, will do so at any opportunity. Few people will abuse privileges. Is this likely to prevent the inappropriate use of materials? Probably not. If the answer is "maybe" or "yes," we still need to examine the potential result on our most important staff members—those who already follow standards or rules before they are even implemented. Thus we will attempt to answer the third question, which is often the most important.

3. *How will my most positive and productive people feel about this policy?* High achievers, which include your superstars and most effective teachers, are often very guilt driven. They are likely to assume that any time a new rule or procedure is implemented, it could be because *they* have done something wrong. When you share with the staff that the copier is being used too much, the high achievers think about that time three years ago when they ran 25 copies for an activity for which they ended up needing

only 22. They are the most likely faculty members to restrict their use of materials or supplies. Is this going to have a productive effect on the school? If you could give one staff member an extra $250 for materials and supplies, which teacher would inspire in you the most confidence that the funds would be used to benefit students? The answer is the same superstars who are most likely to reduce their usage of materials and supplies when a blanket "rule" is implemented.

Restricting the creativity of our most effective teachers will seldom have a positive effect. If, as principal, you wonder how your most effective faculty will receive a new policy, the simplest method is to ask them prior to implementing it. Superstars generally will tell you the truth and not be a part of the rumor mill in a school. If they become involved in spreading gossip and rumors, they will lose respect and not remain superstars. Thus, asking them in advance how they would feel about a new procedure can help answer question number three before the new policy could have a harmful effect on the morale of your most important staff members.

## The Leadership of the Superstar

The key for implementing change and growth in a building is to work with the superstar teachers in the school. If the superstars, the informal leaders, move forward, then the entire building has the opportunity to go with them. If they do not support a change, then it is likely that the change will be minimally successful at best. Although not all informal leaders come from the superstar category, that is a good place to start in determining the potential change agents in a school.

Let's look at an example. One of the school buildings where I was principal was very old and unattractive. Although this was not easy to alter, I felt that the classrooms could appear much more attractive and inviting. I believe that classrooms should look like the best kindergarten classroom you have ever seen. In other words, they should be inviting, comfortable, and have student work displayed all over. Well, my school was quite the opposite and I wondered what to do. I was pretty sure that issuing a memo was not going to have any great effect. So I found a school whose classrooms looked the way I wanted mine to look. They were alive, attractive, and very inviting. This school was also an older facility like mine.

I took three of my superstar teachers with me to a meeting at this school, and I parked at the far end of the building. The entire time we were at the meeting the teachers kept asking me, "Why are we here?" because the meeting did not have much to do with them. Finally, when the meeting ended, we walked out of the meeting room toward the car. I stopped at the first room we walked by and went in. I said excitedly, "Look at this room! This is great!" Well, the three superstars, who were bored to the gourd because of the meeting, grudgingly looked in the classroom and their eyes started to gleam. Then I went into the next room and said, "This one is even better!" My teachers began to have some spring in their step and soon started leading me around and excitedly they went in every classroom in the school. On the way home, they could not stop talking about how attractive and inviting all of the classrooms were. This happened on a Thursday. On Monday, what do you think the three superstars classrooms looked like? Their classrooms did not just emulate the classrooms we had seen the previous week, they looked even better!

In my next weekly staff memo, the *Friday Focus*, I wrote, "Has anybody been in Mary's, Nancy's, or Jackie's rooms lately? Wow! No wonder the kids love their classes. When I went into their classrooms I wanted to bring a sleeping bag and stay all night!" All of my teachers, cooks, custodians, bus drivers, etc. received the *Friday Focus*. What do you think they did the day they read it? Every person in the school went by Mary's, Nancy's, and Jackie's classes to see what they looked like. Even more importantly, other teachers started to change their classrooms' appearance to look like Mary's, Nancy's, and Jackie's.

Contrast this to what would have happened had I taken a couple of backbone teachers or even mediocre teachers with me to that other school. If they had looked at those classrooms on Thursday, what would theirs have looked like on Monday? Probably the same. But even if one of them had changed his or her room, what effect would it have had on anyone else in the school? It is not very likely that it would have been as dramatic as the superstar teachers' impact. Understanding the dynamics and relations in a school is one of the essential elements in successfully working with your difficult teachers. Keep in mind that not all of our difficult teachers are mediocre in the classroom. Some of them are passable classroom teachers—maybe even better than that—but because of their inflexibility, negative influence on other staff members, etc., they may still be difficult teachers to work with. It is beneficial to be mindful of the three categories in which each of your staff members fits, so you can choose opinion leaders to initiate positive change.

## Do Not Give Power to Difficult Teachers

As we proceed in this book, please do not lose sight of the fact that we are going to spend a great deal of time discussing the *least* important people in your school—the difficult teachers. One of the faults in education and educational leadership is that we give too much power to these difficult people. This must stop. It is important that principals consistently remind themselves that the essential people on a faculty are the positive and productive people. Too often we make decisions based on our least important people. Let us look at two examples.

A few years ago I was doing a week-long summer workshop for a school. This school had 45 faculty members. Forty-two of these dedicated educators had voluntarily given up a week of their summer to attend my workshop. Whenever there is a substantial length of time to work with a staff, I try to start out the week with an hour or so of very positive, fun, engaging activities. We got off to a great and productive start, which I felt had set a favorable tone for the week. When we took our first break, one of the teachers from the school approached me. She commented that the first part of the day had gone very well and she was looking forward to the rest of the week. However, she added, the people who need to be here are not here. Then she asked me what should be done. I told her I appreciated her question and asked whether she would be kind enough to ask it in front of the entire group once the break was over.

Sure enough, once everyone returned she raised her hand and said, "We were talking at break that we think this will be a valuable week, but we also feel that the teachers who need to be here are not here. What do you think we should do?"

I paused, looked each person in the eye and said, "I can tell you what I would do. I would praise the Lord. Ask yourself this: If those missing people walked into the room right now, would that make your week better or worse? Would you wave them over to sit by you? Of course not. You would hope they would sit as far away as possible. And so would the other people in here. So let's make sure we do not let these people, who are not even here, ruin *our* week."

The real issue was to examine the amount of power we were going to give to our most negative staff members. We were going to let them ruin our fun week and they were not even there! That is power and we must stop relinquishing it. We must also help all members of our faculty to stop giving power to our most negative staff members.

As principals, when we think about implementing a new program or idea in our school, quite often the first person who comes to mind is that individual whom we know will be most resistant. This is a natural, normal response. However, the real issue is whether we let them prevent our school from improving because of their dispositions.

The second example regarding giving away too much power to our most difficult staff members involves a common habit of some principals. This pertains to making decisions on whether to implement a new concept based on the reaction of the least effective staff members.

I have the good fortune of doing quite a few workshops with principals on supervision, evaluation, and instructional improvement. One of the areas on which we often spend time in these workshops is "differentiated supervision" (Glatthorn). An area of differentiated supervision is self-directed development. This term describes the process of teacher-directed improvement. An example may be goal setting or developing a professional development plan. One idea that I share in self-directed development is that of teachers having themselves videotaped while teaching. Then the teachers watch the video and critique themselves.

This can be accomplished by having a student film crew trained and available. Teachers sign up to have them come in and videotape their classrooms. After they have completed filming the lesson and before the students leave, they eject the tape and hand it to the teacher for them to watch at their own convenience. One of the nice aspects of this idea is that it does not require more work on the part of the principal and it can lead to instructional improvement without adding another responsibility to the building administrator. The point of the story is that when I share this with principals, I will always have someone immediately raise a hand. They share that they cannot implement this program because some of their teachers will not participate in it. And my response is always, "so what?" If we do not do something that can assist some people in our school because a few (or even many) will refuse to do it, then we are giving these resisters a great deal of power and thus limiting the potential of our school.

Another thing to remember is that the first teachers who are likely to take advantage of many opportunities are our superstars. Once they try something and speak highly of it, many of our backbones will also want to participate. If a few others never do, that should not spoil an excellent growth opportunity for a school.

There is an added benefit of superstars often being the risk takers in schools. If they are the first to attempt to implement a new concept, the likelihood of it being successful is much greater than if a less effective staff member attempted the same idea. Thus it is easier to have a positive role model for this idea. They can then provide an example to all other staff, which can be emulated successfully.

# 3

# The Role of the Principal

One of the greatest challenges school leaders face in dealing with negative employees is understanding that it is up to them to address their problems. Most principals are caring people, which is why they choose education as a profession. However, we also know that if the principal does not confront these people, then no one ever will. It is estimated that 15 percent of teachers are marginal. If we consider that there are over 2 million teachers in the United States, this means there are over 300,000 marginal staff who work with students every day! (Podesta, 1996)

Steven Covey has said, "All organizations are perfectly designed to get the results they get." This is true of schools and of every teacher's classroom. Remember in the first section when you were asked whether you could ". . . predict which teacher will send the most students to the office next year?" There is a simple reason that almost every principal can do so with unerring accuracy. If these teachers do not change what they are doing, and our least effective staff members seldom do, then they are going to get the same results regardless of who the students are the next year.

Many studies have been conducted that examine school effectiveness and characteristics of effective principals (Fiore, 1999; Roeschlein, 2002; Turner, 2002; Behling, 1984; Walker, 1990; Ru-

23

therford, 1985). Numerous researchers have concluded that the principal is the decisive element in the effectiveness of a school. During the 1970s, researchers began to focus on differences between "more effective" and "less effective" educational settings. Investigations indicated that the greatest differences in effectiveness occurred at the individual school level. Researchers also began to examine the differences between those schools defined as more effective and schools defined as less effective. One of the most consistent characteristics of an effective school was the existence of a strong instructional leader. Another essential correlate was the existence of a school climate that is safe, orderly, and appropriate for learning to take place. Edmonds (1981) isolated five characteristics that he called correlates of effective schools. He found two of the most important attributes to be (1) the leadership of the school, and (2) the climate of the school. Other researchers have also investigated the relationship between these two characteristics.

Keefe, Kelley, and Miller (1985, pp. 70–71) state that, "in order for a school to be both productive and satisfying, a number of elements must be present. Two, however, emerge as essential: (1) a positive school learning climate and (2) a principal who supports the establishment and maintenance of this climate."

Stronge (1993) describes the importance of unifying the management responsibilities of the principal with instructional leadership duties. He believes that this combination of "educational leadership" provides a healthier paradigm for understanding the principalship. The view draws a relationship between managerial efficiency and instructionally effective schools.

Foriska (1994) discusses instructional leadership as "critical to the development and maintenance of an effective school" (p. 33). The author emphasizes that instructional leaders must influence others to employ the most appropriate instructional practices coupled with their best knowledge of the subject matter. The focus must always be on student learning and principals must readily supply teachers with resources and incentives to keep their focus on students.

Whitaker, Whitaker, and Lumpa (2000) state that an important point to realize is that teachers who are ineffective over a long period of time have been allowed to be. Often their inappropriate methodology is even reinforced. There is little chance they are going to change unless the principal intervenes. It is also critical that principals see that it is their responsibility to cause positive change to occur.

In a study of 163 middle schools in Missouri, T. Whitaker (1997) identified four schools with "more effective" principals and four schools with "less effective" principals. Schools were identified in which principals were one standard deviation above or below the group norm based on teacher responses to the Audit of Principal Effectiveness — a nationally normed assessment of principal skills and teacher responses measured by NASSP's Comprehensive Assessment of School Environments (CASE) instrument. Included in each group of four schools were urban, suburban, small town, and rural schools.

On-site visits and interviews with teachers and the principals were conducted and they revealed three key differences between the more effective and less effective principals. One critical difference between these two groups was that effective principals view themselves as responsible for all aspects of their school. Although these principals regularly involved staff, parents, and others in decision making, they believed it was their responsibility to do whatever was necessary to make their schools the best they could be. The less effective principals were much more willing to "blame" outside factors for problems in their schools.

An example of this difference occurred between the two suburban middle schools. Both were facing significant budget cuts for the upcoming school year. The less effective principal, when discussing the future cuts, chose to be critical of the board members and central office administration. The principal also indicated that there is not much use trying to help kids when others cut your financial support. The teachers in the school echoed the sentiments and disinterest of their leader in making an effort for their students.

At the more positive suburban school, they had just been informed of a much more significant cut than the less positive school. They had a population of 650 students, no assistant principal, and an approximately 30:1 student-teacher ratio. With the cuts, they were losing their only librarian, counselor, and four certified staff, which was going to increase their student-teacher ratio by two to four students per class. Although the leader was very disappointed, a strategy had already been determined that would allow the library to remain open. Implementing a school service project with eighth grade students rotating into the library allowed the library to remain a resource for the school. In addition, the school was going to enhance its advisory program so that as many of the services that the counselors provided could continue to be offered for the students. Although the principal was very disappointed in the budget cuts, the administrator chose to focus solutions to help the students rather than to see the situation as out of control. The teachers shared the same perspective in their interviews.

M. E. Whitaker (1997), in a parallel study involving more and less effective elementary principals in Indiana, asked the following question of the principals, "Who is responsible for the climate in your school?" The more effective principals responded, "I am." The less effective elementary principals responded, "The teachers," "We all are," or "Everybody." These studies not only support the research that the principal is the decisive element in the school, the studies reinforce the fact that the principal is aware that for positive change to occur in the school, it is up to him or her to make sure it happens.

It is also noting that the difference between the more effective principals and less effective principals in working with difficult teachers probably is not that the more effective principals enjoy it. The difference is more likely that the more effective principals roll up their sleeves and do it.

Whitaker (1998), in a study of over 2,000 principals, asked building leaders to compare what things *should* be a priority for them with what things are *actually* a priority in their job as principal. Of the 31 priorities, the principals responded that the tenth highest ranked priority should be to work with less effective teachers. Principals, however, placed working with less effective staff members as 19th on their list of actual practices. One reason for this could be the perceived lack of time by school administrators. These same principals indicated that getting better control over their own time and schedule should be their seventh priority but it was actually their 23rd priority.

A critical aspect of dealing with difficult teachers is that they often consume too great of a proportion of time. We spend a large amount of time and energy working with their discipline problems, building staff morale they have damaged, and developing ways to have a continuously progressive school despite their best resistance efforts.

## Approach Is Everything

The best advice that I ever received as a principal was that you do not have to prove who is in charge, everybody knows who is in charge. And, the more you try to *prove* it, the more people start to wonder. This is especially true when working with the difficult teachers on your faculty. Make sure that you do not treat them in the manner that they treat others. Never raise your voice, use sarcasm, or treat them rudely. It is also critical that we do not take a confrontational or argumentative approach. A simple guideline for working with difficult students in classroom discipline is always to treat students as though their parents were in the room. This same idea applies to working with difficult teachers. Always treat them as though the entire staff were in the room. Realize that your positive and productive teachers want these negative staff members dealt with, but they want it done in a professional manner.

One final piece of advice is to never argue with difficult persons. Realize that they have much more practice at it than you do. Because of their attitude and approach to living, they have spent many hours in their lifetime arguing and they are probably more skilled at that than you are. Sometimes we have to go against our instincts and make sure that we always keep a calm and professional demeanor. The approaches described in this book are all positive non-confrontational approaches that can help lead you and your school along a continual path of growth and improvement.

# Part 2

# Motivating Difficult Teachers

# 4

# Looking for the Good Part—Sometimes You Have to Squint

It may seem futile to offer a section on motivating the most difficult staff members, because you have probably attempted to do this so many times with frustrating results. However, it may be important to revisit motivation in terms of working with these staff members. It is also valuable to keep in mind that opportunities to reinforce or motivate resistant staffers may occur very infrequently. We must become aware of and act upon these chances when they present themselves.

As a principal you should consistently try motivating your most difficult staff members. You should give them every opportunity to improve their behavior. By knowing that you have given them your very best attempt at improvement through motivation, you can feel much more comfortable when you have to approach them in a less positive fashion. Adult decide each day what their frames of mind will be. Teachers make decisions on how they are going to treat each student they work with. You hope that each of your faculty take advantage of the opportunities you provide them.

Leaders look for the opportunity to "catch" someone doing something right. This is a much greater challenge with difficult teachers, because they often do so many things wrong. However, if there is any skill or ability that a difficult staff member does have, make every attempt to take advantage of that. It may not even be directly related to their teaching.

One thing to be aware of is that many teachers have little or no awareness of the effectiveness of their peers' teaching abilities. They feel that if someone is nice to them at lunch they are probably a good teacher. If they have worked with someone who has sent them sympathy cards or shown them personal concern in times of need, then they assume these people are likely to be effective with students. The real issue with this is twofold. First, if you attempt to work with less effective teachers to improve their skills, this may cause a ripple effect with other staff. This is most likely to occur if the other teachers are under the assumption that these ineffective staff members are quality classroom teachers because they are nice interpersonally. The other issue is that these informal relations can cause other staff members to follow their negative lead in resisting change or having a negative influence on the school. Attempting to alter difficult teachers who are held in some regard by their peers is a special challenge and motivation is generally a safe place to start.

Here is an example of a way that motivation may assist in increasing the effectiveness of a difficult teacher who had some informal credibility with other staff members. This particular teacher would readily be described as difficult. This person felt little self-worth and thus had little regard for her students or profession. This challenging staff member did have an uncanny talent for making crafts. If you gave her a soda can, a paper clip, and a piece of yarn she could make the cutest Easter bunny you had ever seen. Her teaching responsibilities had no direct tie into this area and at first I saw it as an annoyance because she focused so much time and energy into her crafts and little or none into teaching. Additionally, because she would make things and give them as gifts or sell them, she had much more credibility with her peers than she otherwise would have. In a way she would buy people's sympathy, or at least rent it, with her non-teaching talent.

Finally, after deciding to effect change in this teacher because of her offensive nature to students, I decided to try to use her one positive talent to cultivate in her a higher energy level. I asked her to make crafts for each of the faculty meetings to use as centerpieces at the tables. We would then use these as door/attendance prizes. Thus, I was able to reinforce her positively for these efforts. Gradually her confidence as a person and professional increased, and over time, she moved from a mediocre to a backbone staff member. Searching for one or two positive traits may help raise a person's feeling of self-worth and allow this to carry over in a positive way to professional performance.

## *Friday Focus*—Developing a Staff Memo that Works

In order to motivate any and all faculty and staff effectively, you must have appropriate tools to work with. In the aforementioned study regarding more effective and less effective elementary principals (Whitaker, M. E., 1997), one of the differences between these groups was that the more effective principals have regular, positive, weekly memos for their faculty and staff. None of the less effective principals produced positive faculty memos on a regular basis.

Knowing the impact that principals have on schools, it is crucial that principals firmly establish individual beliefs and work to effect an appropriate belief system throughout the school. One of the most important and easiest ways to do this is to have a weekly memo.

Whitaker and Lumpa (1995) believe the principal should write this weekly and that it should have several purposes:

1. It should communicate logistical information about upcoming activities and provide a calendar of events. This helps organize the school, but it also allows staff meeting time to be much more positive and productive.

2. The weekly memo should also be used as a staff development tool by consistently keeping the beliefs of the principal in front of the staff. Attaching articles, paragraphs about personal beliefs, etc., are important ways to accomplish this goal. Stronge (1990) felt that one essential role of a principal is to communicate the goals of the school with the faculty and this method of correspondence will enable this to occur on a regular basis. This can help promote growth and direction for all staff including the most difficult staff members.

3. The memo should also be used as a motivational tool. It should be used to mention good things about the school. Examples include everything from, "When I was in Mrs. Johnson's room I was so impressed with . . ." to "I asked four students in the cafeteria on Wednesday what they liked best about school and they said, 'The way the teachers treat us!"

4. The *Friday Focus* can assist with planning. It can help staff members be more prepared for upcoming events because of the information that is regularly provided in the weekly calendar. It can also benefit the planning of the building principal. By regularly including future events, the principal has an early opportunity to organize the logistics of these occurrences. The entire school has the benefit of being more informed and organized.

This weekly memo can be handled in a variety of ways. One effective method is to have one in all teachers' mailboxes when they arrive at work on Friday morning. This way they get a good pick me up on what is typically a difficult work day. The *Friday Focus* enables your faculty meetings to be much more staff development oriented because the routines have been taken care of on paper. If a principal gets in a routine of having these informative, uplifting, and belief focusing memos, the teachers will look forward to it each Friday morning and it will play a critical role in the communication and establishment of the schoolwide belief system for the faculty. These memos can also be routinely sent to central office personnel and to other schools to broaden their impact and to help enhance an awareness of the school's beliefs on a district-wide basis.

It is essential to have as many avenues as possible in order to be able to motivate any staff, but particularly the more resistant members. This concept is critical and this tool will be referred to regularly in upcoming sections of the book. Setting a positive tone for the school is a very important way to help put pressure on negative and resistant staff members.

## Give Difficult Teachers Responsibility

One of the toughest things to do as a principal is to go against our natural instincts, but using this motivational tool requires doing just that. Responsibility is often a powerful motivator for people. This is often true even for the most challenging staff members.

Connie Podesta (1994) feels that it is important that principals realize a couple of things about difficult teachers. One is that the difficult teachers know exactly what they are doing. They work at being difficult. Their behaviors have been reinforced for years. Additionally, it is crucial to note that difficult teachers are rewarded for being difficult. We want to avoid hassles, so we give these teachers easier students, we do not ask them to assume responsibilities, and we give them few extra duties. As a result, they have no incentive to change. Thus, you must demand that they carry a fair share of the load.

The principal's instinct, however, is not to give them responsibilities. There are a couple of reasons why. One is that you assume difficult teachers do not want any responsibility. They seldom meet their expected responsibilities, so why think they would want to do anything additional? But the other more predominant reason principals do not ask them to do any extra tasks is this: they assume they will not do it correctly. After all, they seem to perform so inadequately, there seems little reason to expect they will appropriately attend to any new responsibility.

This is a natural feeling for any principal. For that matter, every productive member of the staff probably shares the same perspective. Yet, giving them a responsibility may be an appropriate way to initiate change in their approach to work.

Realize this responsibility does not have to be the most essential work of the school. Too often we continually rely on our best staff members—often our superstars—to do much of the extra work. There is a good reason for this approach. They will do it right, it will be done on time, and it will be done effectively. However, we need to be very protective of our best faculty members.

One challenge that all principals face is determining when and what to delegate. A quick rule of thumb for this is very simple. A principal should delegate anything that anyone else can do because there are so many things that only the principal can do. This is an easy test to determine whether something should be delegated.

This same test should be applied when we are considering asking our superstars to take on another task. They should only be taking on additional responsibilities that no one else can accomplish. This is again true because there are so many things that *only* your superstars can attain. Thus if you are considering whom to ask to do something extra, you need to decide whether it is essential that your best staff members accomplish it. If it is not, this is an example of something you can share with others.

Giving a difficult teacher responsibility may be particularly effective if it involves peers. Peer involvement can be at a couple of different levels. One example is asking a difficult teacher to coordinate some faculty social responsibilities. If they are aware that their peers know they coordinated this year's Christmas party, or that the other teachers are relying on them to provide the snacks for this month's staff meeting, it may put some additional pressure on them to meet these expectations. The purpose of this is not to embarrass this difficult staff member—quite the opposite. The goal is to have the teacher do something so you can offer thanks and recognition for efforts when the goal is accomplished. Building a feeling of self-value is an essential part of making a difficult teacher feel like a contributing member of the school. This can help move a mediocre teacher to a back-bone or raise the energy level of a challenging staff member to a higher point. The recognition can be a private thank-you or note. It could be a public acknowledgment at a staff meeting or in the *Friday Focus*. This can be a powerful tool to help motivate very reluctant individuals.

A second way to use peers to help motivate your most diffi-cult teachers is a little more complex. It involves linking the chal-lenging teachers with one or more of your most positive staff. Linking a difficult teacher with one or two superstars does two things: It puts pressure on the less effective teacher to perform with this respected person or persons. And it allows the nega-tive faculty member to be a part of something that is very likely to be successful. Most things that a superstar is a part of work out well.

There is an important caveat, however. This process should always begin by asking your superstars if they are willing to participate. You should also explain to them what your purpose is in doing this. Remember, your strongest, most positive staff members are your most important people. Do not sacrifice one of them in order to affect a difficult teacher. Always place the personal regard of your positive, productive staff members first.

Here is an example of giving difficult teachers responsibil-ity by linking them with two superstar teachers. Identify an area of professional development for your staff. A possibility might be cooperative learning. You could locate a workshop for three of your teachers to attend, and have them return prepared to lead some staff development for the entire group. When decid-ing which teachers would be most interested and most effective in presenting to the remainder of the faculty your first thoughts often involve three very effective teachers. Instead of tapping three effective teachers, identify your most exemplary staff mem-ber and ask about any interest in this area. If the response is positive, explain that you would like him or her to be a part of a group of three teachers to attend the workshop and share with other staff members at a future faculty meeting. Then confide that you would like teacher X (a difficult teacher) to be one of the three and explain why.

Explaining why may seem risky. Obviously deciding whether to do so depends on your relationship with the superstar. However, it can be done because a teacher with the high level of respect necessary to be a superstar can probably hold a confidence. Also, if you are pairing a productive teacher with a less effective staff member, it is important that the superstar does not see this as an unfair burden. Explaining your rationale can be validating to this productive teacher. However, if you are uncertain of that trust level, then it may be best to not share your perspective.

Then ask the superstar teacher whom he or she would most like to be the third member of the staff to attend since teacher X is also going to go. This way the superstar is not alone and not uncomfortable. Additionally, teacher X will spend time with two positive teachers and none with often more negative associates. This is an added benefit of structuring this opportunity in this fashion.

Teacher X could then be approached in a couple of different manners. The approach is important; otherwise, the initial reaction may be to say "no." You could share information about the workshop and say you would like teacher X to be a part of the group with the other two members. If the others are respected superstars, this invitation might be viewed positively by teacher X.

You could ask the superstar to approach teacher X, if this would be more effective. Or you could tell teacher X that you and the superstar teacher were visiting about the workshop and considering people who might go and teacher X's name came up. You do not have to expand on this, saying the name was your suggestion.

When the teachers return and lead an inservice for their peers, it may be a wonderful time to praise all three teachers both publicly and privately. You can also repeatedly approach the two positive staff members in private and acknowledge their willingness to attempt to motivate their more reluctant peer.

This motivational process can be especially effective with a negative teacher who is a follower. Staff members who tend to associate with negative leaders and give them an audience, often just want to fit in somewhere. This opportunity may give them the chance to associate with a more positive peer group. Realize that they are weak by nature and will tend to emulate stronger personalities around them.

## Praise in Front of a Superior

The best way to give positive reinforcement to your own son and daughter is to brag about them to another adult. If they overhear this conversation, it is very validating. A similar approach may be just as effective with adults. Praising staff members in front of your superior is a very powerful method to reinforce and motivate faculty. This approach is also valid in working with your difficult staff.

If the superintendent is in your school, take him or her by a difficult teacher's classroom and praise the teacher in front of the superintendent. Say to the superintendent in front of the teacher, "Dr. Smith, I was in Ms. Jones's classroom on Tuesday and she had such an interesting science experiment going on— the kids were so engaged in it—she was doing a terrific job." This, once again, is an example of Steven Covey's (1989) "circle of influence." In the same manner that praising your son or daughter in front of another adult is a powerful reinforcement, praising a teacher in front of one of your superiors can be very valuable to the teacher. The other benefit of praising a mediocre teacher to one of your superiors is that before or after it occurs you can explain to the superintendent why you did it. You can privately acknowledge to the superintendent that although this teacher is often very challenging, you still wanted to recognize your staffer for a positive activity you had observed in their classroom. It may be beneficial to try this method of motivation at least once. If the results are positive, then it is a method that you can implement regularly.

The superior need not be the superintendent. It can be anyone you feel the difficult teacher is most likely to respect. It may be another principal or some other person in or out of the school. Depending on the circumstances, it may be important that it be someone that you have a trusting relationship with so that you can explain what you are hoping to accomplish. Otherwise, the outside person might develop a diminished regard for your professional judgment of staff quality.

# 5

# Public versus Private Praising

Several examples included in the previous chapter involve praising a difficult staff member. Some of the examples entail public praising and others were more private. Praise in the *Friday Focus* is an example of public commendation. When praising difficult teachers, it is important to keep in mind the thoughts and feelings of your positive staff. Be very sensitive to how they will feel when you praise the difficult teachers publicly. They could easily become resentful—and rightfully so.

I feel that a safe rule of thumb is that you have *one* chance to praise a difficult teacher publicly. If you begin to see change or improvement as a result, then you can continue to offer public or private praise at any appropriate opportunity. However, if you observe no change, I feel that you should never offer praise *publicly* again. The reason for this is very simple. The positive people are most important to your school. They will very likely view the public recognition of this difficult teacher negatively. They may feel that their positive efforts are going unrecognized. If there is no change on the part of the teacher, then you cannot continue to offer praise publicly and thereby risk losing credibility with the remainder of the faculty.

This being said, however, the opportunity to give private praise with difficult teachers will continue. This praise can be in whatever form you feel will be most effective. It can also be in a variety of forms and fashions. It is important to understand what praise is. Ben Bissell (1992) has described five things that help praise work. Effective praise is authentic, specific, immediate, clean, and private. Let us apply these general characteristics to the specifics of motivating and praising teachers.

Authentic means that we are genuinely praising people—recognizing them for something that is true. This is an important facet because recognizing something authentic can never grow weary. Sometimes people state that they do not praise more because they feel that it will lose its credibility or that it will become less believable if it happens too much. The way to prevent this is to make sure that it is always authentic. No one ever feels that they are praised too much for something genuine.

Effective praise must be specific. The behavior you acknowledge often becomes the behavior that will be continued. If you can praise difficult teachers' more positive efforts with specific recognition, then you can help them see specific areas of value. For example, acknowledging that teachers effectively used questioning skills during a class that you informally observed can help reinforce that specific area that they do correctly. Sometimes the regard difficult teachers have for themselves is so low that they often feel they can do nothing effectively. Specific praise also allows you to reinforce someone in an authentic manner. You do not have to be dishonest and say they are outstanding teachers, or that lessons were excellent, if they were not. Instead you can identify those areas that did have merit and acknowledge them through praise.

Recognize positive efforts and contributions in a timely manner—with immediacy. Providing authentic and specific feedback soon after it occurs is an important element in making reinforcement effective. One thing that allowed me to give efficient feedback when performing informal "drop-in" supervision (Glatthorn) with several classes in a row, was to take a memo pad with me. If I observed in eight classes for two to five minutes each, I would remain in the last class and write specific words of praise for each of the eight teachers, assuming that there was something authentic I could reinforce. When I returned to the office, I would give the notes to the secretary and ask that the notes be put in the teachers' mailbox. Other principals carry Post-it notes with them and put them on the door when they leave individual classes. You could also place them on the teacher's desk, grade book, or lesson plan book for even more immediate feedback. I would work very hard to find something positive as often as possible in teachers' classrooms. It could be related to the topic, what students were saying or doing, the physical environment, or even a new tie a teacher wore. Positive reinforcement is a valuable change tool.

The fourth praise guideline for praise is that it be clean. Clean praise is just that—praise offered honestly without qualifiers or caveats or provisions. This is often a very challenging requirement for praise, especially for educators. Clean means a couple of different things. Praise that is not *clean* is issued in order to get the teacher to do something in the future. In other words, it is important to compliment teachers because it is authentic, not just because you are hoping that they will do something different tomorrow. Remind yourself of this quite regularly. If you do not, you will be tempted to discontinue praising, because you will feel it "does not work." An example of this would be if you praise difficult staff members for the "wait time" they were using in class during the morning and then later in the day they are their usual rude selves to you. Do not feel that these two events are linked. Often we take the surly manner of difficult teachers and others very personally. Though our goal is to get them to discontinue this approach, we need to be aware that more often their mood has much more to do with them and the way they feel about themselves than it does with you and how they are regarding you.

Clean praise cannot include the word "but." For example, if you are trying to compliment someone and say, "I appreciated the tone of voice you were using with Steven today, but, have you changed your bulletin boards lately?" The individual you hoped you were praising will very likely only remember the part after the "but," which was a criticism and very unlikely to recall the attempted compliment at the start of the sentence. If you really mean to praise someone, then it is important to divide these two events. If you stopped with, "I appreciated the tone of voice you were using with Steven today," then this could have been an authentic, specific, immediate, positive, and clean reinforcing event for this teacher. This helps establish two things for this difficult teacher. It helps clarify the expectations you have for the manner in which the teacher works with students. It also develops a baseline for both of you that the teacher is *able* to treat students appropriately. It will be much easier to revisit this positive event later, if needed.

The other part of the comment, "Have you changed your bulletin boards lately?" has no need for immediacy. Tying these two together reduces or even eliminates the value of the praise. With difficult people, opportunities to praise are rarer than are opportunities to be critical. Another issue to remember is this: Most difficult people will probably make similar errors chronically. If you pass up the opportunity to comment today, feel confident that their bulletin board will still need some updating tomorrow.

Dr. Bissell believes that most praise should be private. I agree with this and would also say that if in doubt, you are always safe to praise someone in private. As previously mentioned, difficult people offer few deeds that should receive public praise, if they do not change. You must protect the feelings of your productive backbones and superstars. However, if all praise is given in private, then you might miss many teachable moments. This is true when it involves difficult teachers and it can also apply when you attempt to alter the behavior of the majority of staff members.

Recall the example regarding having three superstars attend a meeting at a school whose appearance I was hoping our classrooms could emulate? We went to the meeting and started peeking into classrooms and then the superstars altered their own room appearances over the weekend. Having three teachers improve the appearance of their classrooms is a benefit to your school and particularly to those three classes. But, as mentioned earlier, those three superstars' classes probably needed the least upgrading in appearance of any classrooms in the school. However, the remainder of the faculty became involved because of the *public* recognition given them in the *Friday Focus*. This allowed their impact to go well beyond their three classrooms. And, eventually, these changes even positively impacted some of my mediocre teachers. Without public praising, the impact would have been much more limited.

Public praising can also be used on rare occasions with difficult staff. Several examples will be given in future chapters, but the one cited previously regarding giving them responsibility is an application of this concept. If difficult staff members are aware that coworkers know that they are responsible for a task, then there is already some public recognition of this. If they come through, the praise being public is often very appropriate and effective in changing future behaviors.

The example of the teacher making crafts for the faculty meeting is a second one involving the public praising of a difficult staff member. Without the public recognition of efforts, I am confident that the positive results would have been greatly diminished.

Before leaving this concept of public praising, however, keep in mind that superstars want autonomy *and* recognition. This recognition does not necessarily mean only public acknowledgments, but it is important to not lose sight of this when considering the public praising of the difficult or mediocre staff. Be mindful that one of the most important aspects of being a superstar is being respected by others—including your peers. So also be aware of the amount of public recognition you give your superstars, especially if positive reinforcement is somewhat new to your school climate and culture. If the other staff become resentful of public praise for the superstars they are likely to respect them less. Then they are no longer superstars and this is a dramatic limitation on their future abilities to help be a positive influence for the school.

An easy test of whether it is acceptable to praise in public is whether it is something anyone *could* have done. In the next section there is an example of publicly recognizing a teacher who chose to write a grant that would benefit the school. Any staff member could have chosen to pursue a grant and thus could have received this recognition. This was proven true in the future when many others joined the previous efforts in pursuing other grants. These grant-writing efforts even included a couple of former mediocres and challenging staff! Thus, there became many other appropriate opportunities for positive reinforcement in an authentic, specific, immediate, clean, and public manner.

# Part 3

# Making Difficult Teachers Uncomfortable

# 6

# Uncomfortable Is Good

If difficult teachers never feel uncomfortable, they will never change. Imagine a teacher who has been employed for 37 years. However, instead of having 37 years of experience, the person has only one year of experience 37 times. These teachers most likely have been allowed to teach in this same fashion over and over.

Ineffective teachers cannot be allowed to come to work and feel happy with their job performance. If ineffective teachers feel no discomfort, then they will continue to operate in the same fashion forever. And remember, ineffective teachers will probably never quit, because they lack other career options. So what should a principal do? Allowing ineffective faculty to feel comfortable gives them permission to continue to perform ineffectively.

An easy check for a principal as to whether a decision is sound is to ask this question: "If I do this, which teachers will like this decision and which ones will not?" If you determine that your superstars will probably not like a decision, then you probably should not make it. However, if some of your difficult staff will not support it then that might or might not be cause for concern. With each decision and in each situation, ask yourself, "Who will be more comfortable and who will be less comfortable?" Determining the answer to this question can be a great benefit before proceeding with the implementation of a decision.

If you ask superstars their opinion about something, they usually have one and they will often share it with you. Additionally, they have high levels of professionalism, which includes the ability to be confidential. Including these people in making decisions is an essential part of being an effective principal.

Whitaker (1997) found that the more effective Missouri middle school principals identified key informal teacher-leaders and used them in decisionmaking. They shared two reasons for doing this. The first is that their decisions would not be accepted by the faculty without the support of these informal leaders. This supports the Vroom and Yetton model that one of the important aspects of an effective decision is its acceptance (Vroom and Jago, 1988). The second reason is that these key faculty members often offered very insightful opinions and accurate perceptions as to what solutions really were best.

The more effective principals were able to identify immediately the key informal leaders of their schools and they were able to indicate why they felt these teachers were the leaders. The less effective principals tended to rely on other administrators or no one for input and feedback rather than teachers. None of the principals at the four less effective schools were able to readily identify key teacher-leaders to whom they went for input and feedback before making decisions.

Staff input is essential to an effective school. Both formal and informal input opportunities are appropriate as long as key staff members are involved in participative management and decision making. This supports the view of many researchers (Purkey and Smith, 1982; Snyder, Krieger, and McCormick, 1983; Lipham, 1981; Garten and Valentine, 1989; Keefe, Clark, Nickerson, and Valentine, 1983; Danley and Burch, 1978; Webster, 1994; McEwan, 1994; Harris, 1997; and Lashway, 1998.)

The effective principals shared two main reasons why they regularly went to their superstars for input before making decisions. The first was that if their superstars were not going to support a decision, there was little chance that it would be supported by the majority of the faculty. The second reason was that if the superstars did not think something was a good idea, there was a really good chance that it was not a good idea. Checking with these key staff members is a valuable method of avoiding ineffective decisionmaking.

It is also valuable to remember that superstars want two things—autonomy and recognition. The desire for autonomy is one reason that you should seldom try to control your ineffective staff members by implementing rules that affect all teachers. Your positive and professional staff members will follow the guidelines and your difficult teachers will not. Then what happens is your positive members just get more upset at the difficult teachers because once again, they are not following the rules.

## Raising Discomfort Levels

There are several effective methods to raise the discomfort level among difficult teachers. These methods include: empowering the good guys, raising their interpersonal intelligence level, using effective approaches at faculty meetings, reducing negativity in the teachers' workroom, making teachers accept responsibility for their situations, and using peers to help make them more uncomfortable. Always assuming that difficult teachers want to do what is right is also very productive, because it allows us to maintain relations with the challenging staff members at the same time that we are helping them grow by making them uncomfortable.

Relationships are everything to an effective principal. Developing skills in making teachers uncomfortable does not require damaging relations with difficult teachers. It also does not harm in any way the critical relations you establish and nurture with many positive staff members. These approaches can allow them to maintain their dignity while at the same time challenging negative faculty to grow as people and as educators.

## Empower the Good Guys

One method to begin to make less effective faculty feel uncomfortable is to empower the effective teachers on a staff. In other words, empower the superstars and positive staff members. This can help to make the less effective people feel like they are missing out on something. It is also important to recall that it is best to draw public recognition to accomplishments when it is something any one *could* do. Here is an example of positive empowerment.

Shortage of funds is an issue almost every school and administrator faces. One way to acquire additional resources is through the pursuit of outside grant funding. This was a goal that I had as a principal and yet none of my staff had ever written any grants. After much discussion and encouragement, one of my best teachers decided to attempt writing a grant for a new program. As often happens, the deadline was fast approaching and the grant was not done. The teacher, who was a very high achiever, was becoming somewhat overwhelmed by the prospects of not completing the application. I told her that I would hire a substitute teacher for her for a day so that she could work on the grant. She was very relieved and asked whether she should work at home that day so no one would see her having a substitute. I told her quite the opposite. I would like to have her at school working in the teachers' workroom so that everyone could see her. It was important for all staff to understand that we try to reinforce the extra efforts that faculty make. This was also an effort that could support public praising, because it was something everyone *could* have done. This is one of the exceptions to the private praising guideline.

Another way to empower the good guys is to recognize consistently positive faculty contributions and efforts in your *Friday Focus*. This is another way to empower every staff member who makes positive strides in the school. Again, your goal is not only to spotlight a few people or to ignore certain people. Instead, it is to regularly acknowledge the positive contributions of any and all staff members. When some difficult teachers (or other employees) begin to notice that their names seldom appear in the *Friday Focus*, they might decide to ask you why. This is a great conversation starter. Calmly reply, "I try to acknowledge any *positive* contributions that I see here at our school." This is a powerful way to begin a discussion of the types of things that staff members can do to be recognized for their efforts. Because they are generally things that anyone could do, every staff member can choose to contribute in a positive fashion and feel valued.

# 7

# Accept Responsibility— They Can't Pass the Buck

## Interpersonal Intelligence

The contributions of Howard Gardner's (1993) work in the area of multiple intelligences are many. However, one particular concept that applies to difficult teachers requires an understanding of the terms *intrapersonal* intelligence and *interpersonal* intelligence. The prefix *intra* means within. Part of the concept of intrapersonal intelligence is how well a person knows himself; i.e., strengths and weaknesses. The prefix *inter* means between. One aspect of interpersonal intelligence is how well people are able to determine how they are received by others. In other words, interpersonal intelligence is a sense of how you are coming across to the people with whom you are communicating.

Although difficult teachers often have many different characteristics, one similarity that a great number of less effective teachers share is low interpersonal intelligence. They do not have a feel or sense of how they are coming across to the people with whom they are communicating. An example of this is a teacher who is a poor lecturer and yet the teacher persists in lecturing as a primary mode of teaching. To an outsider or even to the students, it is obvious that few people pay attention, understand, or care what the teacher is saying. Yet, the teacher has no awareness of how poorly students respond.

A second example is a staff member who has very poor body language in interactions with others. A principal knows that as soon as parents meet this teacher the parents will want their child to be moved from that teacher's class. People who display poor body language roll their eyes, put their hands on their hips, speak sarcastically, and listen poorly.

A third example includes faculty members about whom everyone always says, "Don't they know that nobody likes them? Aren't they aware that when they walk into a room everyone else scrambles to leave? Can't they see that no one values their comments at staff meetings?" The answers are no, no, and no. They lack the interpersonal intelligence to be able to interpret the messages that others are sending them.

It is also important to be aware of the fact that often people have responded to these teachers in the same manner their whole career—often throughout their lives. Let us take for example, the teacher who is a boring lecturer. When the teacher looks out over the class, several students are sleeping and students have issued bored looks. This scene has been repeated regularly for 26 straight years. Why would the teacher expect to see something different? Teachers with poor body language have always had parents respond rudely. Each year several parents request or demand that their children be transferred from the poor teachers' classes after parents meet the ineffective teachers at open houses or back-to-school night. Why would they be shocked that it happens year after year?

The third example given was the faculty member whom others do not like. If people are rude and overbearing at work, they probably are at home also. More than likely they have been that way their entire lives. They are used to people responding to them in a cold or disinterested way. This is the response they have received for years.

So, what do principals do? The principal has to provide the difficult teachers' interpersonal intelligence. Principals must share with them how they are coming across. They have to communicate with them how they are being received. Principals have to advise them regarding the messages their demeanors are sending.

I once knew a counselor with poor interpersonal intelligence. One day when walking past his office, I noticed he was with one of the nicest girls in the school and her mother. These were wonderful people who unfortunately had a family crisis . They were visiting with the counselor primarily because they just wanted someone to talk to. There was a box of tissues between them, and it was obvious the mother and daughter were both very emotional. While glancing in I noticed that the counselor was leaning back in his chair, yawning, and looking at his watch. The message this was sending was obvious. After the mother and daughter left I shared the following with the counselor. "Jim, when I walked by your office while you were visiting with Kim Smith and her Mother, I was offended when I saw you lean back in your chair, look at your watch, and yawn. My feelings were hurt. How do you think they felt?"

Another example of providing interpersonal intelligence is helping staff understand how they are coming across. One day at a start-of-the-year open house, I was in the hall and saw two parents walking out of a teacher's room with their hands on their hips, furrowed brows, and sour expressions on their faces. I thought they were very upset. Then it hit me. They were imitating the teacher they just saw. I felt like it was my responsibility to communicate with this very difficult teacher what I had witnessed. This needs to be done in a nonthreatening manner, but it needs to be communicated. If the principal does not do it, there is little chance it will happen. A gentle way to do this is to say to the teacher, "I am telling you this because I would want to know." You are not trying to attack the teacher, you are trying to halt the offensive behavior.

It is critical that the principal impart interpersonal intelligence to those teachers who lack this skill. A great way to help build your self-confidence to do this is to ask yourself, "If I were doing something that was regularly offensive to the people around me would I want to know?" If the answer is, "yes,"—and with effective people it is—then the principal must provide this knowledge.

## Accepting Responsibility— They Cannot Pass the Buck

Just as effective principals accept responsibility for all that happens in the entire school, effective teachers must accept responsibility for all that occurs in their classrooms. If the best teachers in a school give tests or homework assignments and the kids do poorly on them, whom do the teachers blame? They blame themselves. They wonder whether they did not spend enough time on the lesson or if they did not explain it well enough. They examine themselves and what they did. They accept the responsibility for the poor performance of their students.

If the least effective teachers in a school give homework assignments or tests and the students do poorly, whom do they blame? They blame the students, parents, lack of administrative support, or maybe even last year's teachers! Instead of looking at themselves—at behavior they can change—they look to pass that responsibility to someone else. This also gives them an excuse not to change their behavior.

You must work toward teachers becoming more aware of their own responsibility to influence the student behaviors. When teachers consistently have students who arrive late at class, very often they are the same teachers whose classes *you* are not in a hurry to visit either. Helping those teachers realize they determine what happens in their classrooms is an important role for the principal. If teachers continually blame someone else, then they are letting themselves off the hook of being responsible to their students. Assuming and accepting this role of influence is essential in improving many less effective staff members.

Getting the less effective teachers to accept responsibility for student learning, behavior, and interest in their classes is an important element in improving teacher performance. Stephen Covey (1989) describes this acceptance as moving from a person's circle of concern to a person's circle of influence. In other words, moving away from something we cannot affect to moving toward something that we can affect. This is an important factor in working with more staff members.

My interest in acceptance of responsibility stemmed from becoming principal of a school in which many of the teachers, particularly the less effective ones, consistently voiced their opinions that, "Maybe I could teach these students something, if last year's teachers had taught them better." Not only do these sentiments create a divisive atmosphere in a building, they truly relieve the current teacher from responsibility for student performance. Many opportunities exist to help staff members realize that they are responsible for the success of their classes. One of the most important is establishing the expectation that they do not pass that responsibility onto others over whom they have little or no control.

We decided as a staff that we would not be critical of previous teachers or schools. We realized that there was nothing we could do about them anyway, so we felt that it was not beneficial to be critical of things outside our circle of influence. With this framework in mind, let us take a look at a couple of things you can do to assist teachers to take responsibility.

Be very clear with the faculty in a positive tone that you are not going to be critical of outside influences that you have no influence over. Discuss this from the perspective that entering a "blame" mentality will lead to frustration and drain the energies from areas where you and your staff can impact students.

To help reinforce this one time, I adapted an anonymous poem to fit the needs of our school, shared it at a faculty meeting, and included a copy with our *Friday Focus* so that everyone could have this reminder. You might consider preparing something similar.

## PASSING THE BUCK DOWN THE LINE
*Adapted by Todd Whitaker*


Said the college professor,
"Such rawness in the student is a shame,
Lack of preparation in high school is to blame."

Said the high school teacher,
"Good heavens, that boy's a fool.
The fault, of course, is with the
Junior High School."

The junior high teacher noted,
"It's so hopeless and sad
Thanks to those elementary clowns,
They can't subtract or add."

The grammar school teacher said,
"From such stupidity
May I be spared.
They sent him up to me so unprepared."

The primary teacher huffed,
"Kindergarten blockheads all.
They call that preparation?
Why, it's worse than none at all."

The kindergarten teacher said,
"Such lack of training never did I see.
What kind of parents
Must those kids' parents be?"

This responsibility to teach
Is something that we all share,
But somehow the grass is
Always greener over there.

So rather than hand down
These grumbles and groans,
Let's remember about glass houses,
And the throwing of stones.

The answer of course,
It is not chance or luck
But what we do in our own classes,
So let's not pass the buck.

A couple of other events occurred that also helped staff members keep their focus on accepting responsibility for the performance and behavior of the students in their classrooms. One involved a language arts teacher who consistently complained about how the students would not do work anymore. One day she stopped me when I was walking down the hall and she said, in her usual disgusted tone, "These kids here will not do homework. I gave 28 kids an assignment last night and three turned it in!" In a very calm manner I asked her to tell me what the assignment was. She described it to me. I then shared with her that coincidentally I had just left Mrs. Smith's classroom (a superstar) and she had given the exact same homework assignment the night before. I went on to tell this teacher that Mrs. Smith has 28 students also and 27 of her students turned in the assignment. I then asked this complaining teacher what she felt the difference was. Her initial response was that she had no idea.

I reminded her that in developing class rosters the students in our school are randomly mixed. I added that she and Mrs. Smith each had 28 students, and that the teachers gave the same homework assignment. Yet, in Mrs. Smith's class, 27 of 28 students did the work and in her class 3 of 28 students did the work. This led to a very valuable discussion about accepting responsibility for her students' performance and that she is the decisive factor in the classroom. This was a valuable growth experience for this difficult staff member. From that point forward she was able to focus her energies more productively on what she could do differently. She had moved back into her circle of influence.

Another valuable opportunity arose when I was a middle school principal. We were having a science department meeting, and the high school science chair, Mr. Rogers, attended. He was a very bright individual and an effective teacher—one whom I would have loved to have in my school. However, this particular day he was not in the best mood. He had just left a science department meeting at his school in which the freshmen science teachers were saying that the ninth grade students would not do their homework because the middle school teachers were not strict enough with them the prior year. The middle school teachers, who for the most part shared the belief that we do not criticize previous teachers, wondered how I would respond to this concern, which was an example of what we no longer did at our school.

I asked Mr. Rogers whether he were a good student in high school. He proudly responded, "Yes, I was a very good student." Knowing the answer to the questions before I even asked them, I proceeded even further. I then asked Mr. Rogers if he were a good student in college. He thrust out his chest and replied, "I was an excellent student in college!" I then asked him, "Did you try to the best of your ability in every single college class you ever had?" Mr. Rogers at first exclaimed, "Yes!" But he hesitantly added, "Well, except for this one philosophy class I had. That professor was quite a deal." So I asked Mr. Rogers, "In that philosophy class, when the teacher gave an assignment, did you race over to the library and work until all hours of the night doing your very best?" He responded quickly, "No, not in that class. I blew it off." So I asked Mr. Rogers, "Was that because your high school teachers were not strict enough with you?"

"Why no, I did not try very hard in the philosophy class because I did not respect the professor," he responded with his voice trailing off. I paused and then said. "Would you mind sharing this story with your freshmen science teachers." It made the point that it is essential to understand that we must accept responsibility as teachers for what occurs in our classrooms. This is a critical skill which often differentiates effective teachers from less effective staff members.

The importance of accepting responsibility is very broad-based. It applies to the variety of behaviors of students in the classroom. Effective classroom managers seldom rely on the principal, assistant principal, or other resources for changing student behavior in their classrooms. It also applies to the area of student achievement, test scores, and assessments. Effective teachers also assume more responsibility in initiating contact and communicating with students' parents and family members. Establishing acceptance of responsibility as an expectation and as a part of the culture of a school is important for an educational leader.

# 8

# The Teachers' Lounge and Other Challenges

## Faculty Meetings

I believe that faculty meetings are critical to effective schools. In a study of more effective and less effective elementary principals and school climates, M. E. Whitaker (1997) determined that in more effective schools, teachers looked forward to and valued faculty meetings. The converse was true in the less effective settings.

In many schools, negative staff members with strong personalities intimidate some of the other faculty. In addition, the principal is often uncomfortable or, at times, even unnerved by these people. Feeling discomfort or intimidation is not pleasant for the building administrator. However, if principals keep in mind how uncomfortable they feel, they can easily imagine how the other teachers and staff in the school feel.

In faculty meetings all staff develop a sense of these informal— often uncommunicated—dynamics. It is critical that these important opportunities be productive and positive. They are an essential part of establishing the proper school culture and climate.

Where do difficult teachers often sit at faculty meetings? In asking hundreds of groups of school administrators this question, three responses consistently arise. The difficult people sit *together*, *in the back*, and *near the door*. If any or all of these three elements are true in your school, ask yourself, "Who are the most comfortable people in the room?"

Think of attending church on Sunday. Which rows fill up first? People who arrive early will often sit in the back rows. When I became principal of a school with several challenging staff members, we did not have merely one table of malcontents; they had to push several together. I thought that if I was uncomfortable at staff meetings how do my good teachers feel? Historically the majority of teacher comments at the staff meetings were negative and the positive members seldom contributed. I knew I had to address this problem. I will explain how I did it shortly. However, I would like to take you through a scenario first.

Let us say that at a faculty meeting you have some staff members who express concerns about student discipline and/or behavior. One of your superstars, sitting in the middle of the room or toward the front, raises her hand and says, "I think we should start a lunch detention program. We could use an empty classroom near the cafeteria, and kids who have not behaved appropriately at school could eat their lunch in that room to take away the social element for a day. It would be immediate, we would not have to worry about transportation before or after school with the students, and taking them away from their peers is very effective." Then she added, "We could easily do this if every staff member volunteered to give up their lunch one day a month to supervise this lunch detention room."

If this occurred in your meeting, how would your difficult teachers react? There would be moaning, laughing, or maybe even sarcastic comments such as, "You look like you need to give up lunch!" The real question is, "Who is the least comfortable person in the room at this time?" Your superstar is; and this has to change.

As the principal with difficult people sitting at faculty meetings together, in the back, and near the door, I realized that if the dynamics within our staff meeting were going to be different, it was up to me to alter them. Traditionally our staff meetings were conducted in the media center/library using the table arrangement that was in place for the school day (Figure 1). Additionally, there were many more chairs than there were staff members. Thus, not only did the more negative people sit in the back, everyone was spread out over quite a physical distance. I quickly realized that I was going to be uncomfortable in the staff meetings. And if I as principal felt uncomfortable, how would other teachers feel?

One other thing that I noticed was that even though most people would prefer to sit in the back row at a meeting—and my most difficult people arrived at the meeting last—the other more positive teachers would not take their chairs. Instead, they left their seats open for them. It was like these seats were emotionally "saved" for these negative staff members. Now that was informal power. The question I faced was how do I alter this dynamic?

After putting much thought into it, I decided to rearrange the media center right before each staff meeting. I turned the chairs and tables around so that the traditional back was the front and the front was the back. We removed all the extra chairs to establish as much physical closeness as possible. Also, the chairs were arranged in an opera-house style with each chair facing the front (Figure 2). Generally the most difficult people come in last. With this new arrangement the difficult people did not have their "reserved section" so now as other staff members entered the room they filled the chairs up starting in the back. Then as the more negative staff filed into the room with this new arrangement, the only seats that were open were right down front. The more negative staff were sitting in the front of the room and they were the most uncomfortable people in the room. Then, in following with my nonconfrontational style, at the start of the meeting I said with a genuine smile on my face, "Isn't it neat to have change once in a while? I thought we could give this arrangement a try." Then we would start the meeting. Removing negative faculty from their comfort zone caused them to be much quieter and less willing to voice their confrontational opinions in staff meetings.

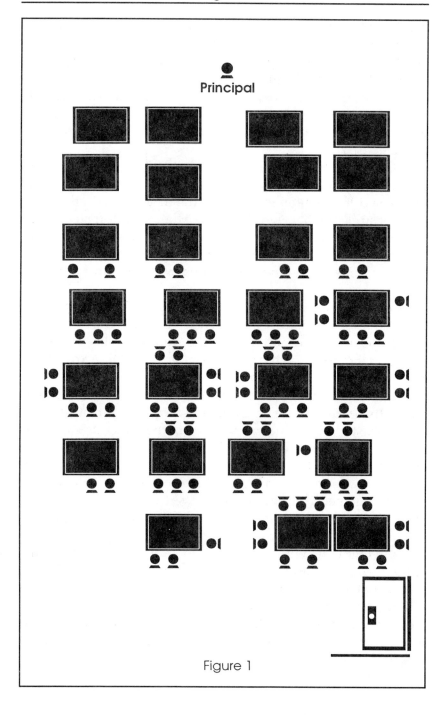

Figure 1

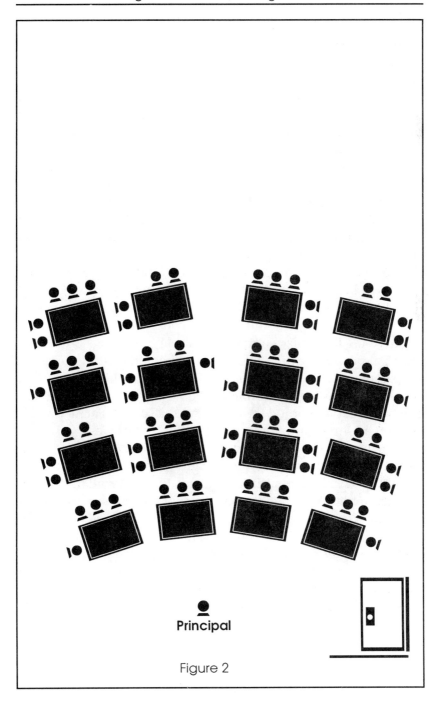

Principal

Figure 2

After a couple of meetings I once again reversed the room from back to front and front to back, but this time I left it in the opera-house style and continued to remove all of the extra tables and chairs. However, I permanently eliminated the two back tables which had once been the domain of the negative staff. I pushed the two tables together, took away the chairs from around them, and put the cookies, snacks, and beverages on the tables (Figure 3). After all, shouldn't the food be near the door?

One final strategy: At staff meetings I would have my assistant principal come into the room last and he would sit next to the most vocal negative staff member we had. When he sat down, he would very nicely ask this difficult teacher, "Is this seat taken?" and sit there for the meeting. The most negative person became the most uncomfortable person in the room and was also the least likely to make negative comments at the meeting.

It is ironic, but as principals we would not think twice about sitting next to a positive teacher at a meeting, but there is something uncomfortable about seating yourself next to the most negative faculty. This is another example of how we often give informal power to difficult teachers. When other staff members are present, they observe this dynamic also. Taking away that power and making the difficult people uncomfortable is very important in developing the culture of the school. Faculty meetings are an important and visible part of that process.

A principal should also think of the room dynamics, seating, etc., at each committee or small group meeting. Do you have any staff that elect to sit in a chair against the wall and away from the table? Are there any faculty that will consistently sit as far away from you as possible? Room arrangement and how you choose to locate yourself can dramatically impact the productivity of any meeting. Everything we do affects climate. It is up to you to decide whether you are going to attempt to impact that climate or let it evolve randomly.

It is also important to develop these same strategies and skills in positive teacher-leaders. Their awareness of faculty dynamics can be very beneficial in the development of their effective leadership skills. The knowledge and skills of your positive staff members help support your school in a productive manner.

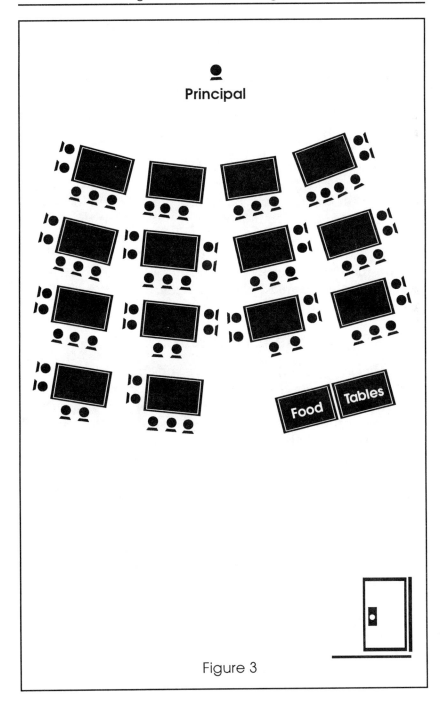

Figure 3

Faculty meetings also provide an opportunity for the principal to model how to work appropriately with difficult teachers. The approach we take with difficult staff members will demonstrate to the rest of the faculty how to remain in control and how to avoid arguments and power struggles. This will be a valuable tool for the positive staff members to observe. It will allow others in the school to use these effective strategies with negative peers.

If the dynamics of faculty meetings are so ingrained that only negative teachers share opinions, then privately approaching superstars and other respected teachers to ask them to contribute can assist in the alteration of the established climate. Reducing the level of comfort of the negative staff can and will increase the comfort of the positive faculty members. Asking some of your positive teacher-leaders to contribute voluntarily at the staff meetings can more quickly help less assertive, productive staff be more willing to share and participate.

## The Teachers' Workroom

Higher education has many faults and critics. Many of these complaints and concerns about higher education are justified. However, I can confidently state that no college or university teacher education program of which I am aware has a course on griping in the teachers' lounge. And yet, too often, new teachers begin to develop this habit by November of their first year. What is the most reliable predictor of whether teachers will complain in the teachers' lounge next week? It is whether they complained in the teachers' lounge this week. This type of behavior becomes a habit that builds upon itself. If there is no intervention or attempt to alter this course, then this negative griping begins to affect the tone and morale of the entire staff and school.

At many schools, the dialogue in a teachers' workroom, lunchroom, or lounge often turns into regular gripe sessions. These complaints may be about the school board, central office, the principal, another teacher (who, of course, is not present), parents, or even worse, students. Many times the conversations may be about some combination of all of these things. The worst thing about a school that develops an environment like this is that negative attitudes and tones start to wear down positive faculty and eventually infiltrate into our classrooms by causing less positive attitudes about work. Principals must make efforts to alter this inappropriate practice in their school.

How can this be accomplished? Obviously there is no guaranteed way, but I would like to share a story that I shared with my staff at the start of every school year. This story has also been shared with and received positively by hundreds of other teachers in other schools.

> The teachers' lounge is a place to relax, socialize, enjoy each other's company, and maybe even every once in a while, a place to get some work done. But it is never a place where we criticize central office, run down administration, berate parents, criticize each other, or ever, ever belittle students. And there are two reasons that we do not do this. One is that we cannot be in such an environment, and leave that environment and be as effective with the young people we work with as we need to be. The second reason is that my life is too short and I do not get paid enough to dread going to work every day. If I am in an environment like that—where people are whining, complaining, and moping—then I do not enjoy going to work. As I look around this room I do not see anyone who gets paid so well or whose life will be so long that they can afford to dread going to work each day.

This is a very powerful message to communicate to your staff. Whenever I share this with faculties there are a couple of interesting reactions. When I share the first reason—that we cannot be in an environment like that and leave that environment and be as effective in our classrooms as we need to be—the positive teachers in the school love to hear it and often start applauding. They have been wanting someone to address this issue for all the years they have been in education. It is a very empowering message and it validates the beliefs of your positive staff. Since the positive staff members are your most important faculty, this, in and of itself, is enough benefit.

However, I also want to share a reason for the naysayers. The second part of the message is for them—that our lives are too short and we do not get paid enough to dread going to work and if we are around people who complain all of the time then it is not much fun to go to work. Do I think that this one communication eliminates all teachers' lounge talk? Of course not, but I do think it does several things. The first is that it can help establish a standard for how we approach our jobs each day. The second is that it can help break the cycle of coming to work every day and complaining about something. A third benefit is that it may prevent others from joining in on the gripe cycle. A fourth benefit is that it reinforces your positive people by reminding them that their beliefs are correct. And a fifth benefit is, when you share this expectation and everyone in the room turns and stares at the leading gripers in the school, these negative staff members may become the most uncomfortable people in the room.

## Use Peers—Use Caution

Using peers to effect the behavior of difficult teachers is sometimes walking a very fine line. However, it might have a powerful and significant impact in a way that no other approach can.

I have mentioned pairing up a difficult teacher with one or two superstars and having them attend a workshop. Together they would provide training or inservice to the rest of the faculty. Linking the less effective staff member with the superstar(s) assured that the results would be positive. It allowed for a potentially increased positive relationship between the mediocres and the superstars. It also provided an excellent opportunity for reinforcement of a difficult teacher. This could be either private, public, or both.

However, this section is subtly or not so subtly using peer pressure. By using peers, I am not approaching this in the sense of asking other teachers to deal with the person. That is not the responsibility of other staff members. Dealing with the less effective faculty is the responsibility of the principal. I have heard many principals at all levels express the thought, "Why don't any of the other teachers say anything to them? Why don't they stand up to them? Why do my positive people allow the negative people to intimidate them?" My response to that is this: It is not up to the other teachers to do that. That is not *their* responsibility, it is the responsibility of the *principal*. Revisiting Steven Covey's circle of influence (1989), indirectly and informally using peer pressure can be very effective.

Difficult teachers often emotionally distance themselves from many facets of their work. They rationalize that the kids are different today or that if parents would discipline them at home, maybe the teachers could be effective. They also emotionally distance themselves from administration. They may feel that central office does not pay them what they deserve (which of course is true—they are receiving too much!). They might also believe the principal is picking on them, does not support them, or is out to get them, etc. Often this emotional distancing is very much a defense mechanism. By using these excuses, they avoid looking at their own flaws. Clearly, this is not a healthy approach. Many times difficult teachers do not completely disconnect themselves from their peers.

Your initial reaction to this may be, "Oh, yes they have. They do not care what their coworkers think of them." Before settling completely on that diagnosis, ask yourself a few questions about difficult teachers. I want you to think beyond how they would answer these questions publicly. Showing regard for how others view them might contrast to their visible persona. Unhappy people often work very hard at protecting their own feelings, even if they show little regard for the feelings of others. Because of their emotional distancing and self-protective approaches, their public responses to these questions may be different than their private thoughts. However, attempt to delve deeper into their minds and comprehend what they really think and feel; do not limit yourself to how they would respond. Pretend each of your difficult teachers were answering these questions:

- Do you care if the other teachers in this school like you?

- Do you care if the other teachers in this school respect you?

- Do you hope that the other teachers in this school perceive you as effective?

- Do you hope that when you retire your coworkers will hold you in high regard?

Would they answer any of the above questions "yes"? Score one point for each question to which the honest answer would be, "yes."

Again, imagine the difficult teacher answering these questions honestly:

- Do you hope other teachers in the school laugh at you behind your back?

- Do you hope that the other teachers dread doing committee work with you?

- Do you want the other teachers to wish you were not in their grade level, on their team, or in their department?

- Do you hope that other teachers do not want to have their classroom next to yours?

- Do you wish that your peers hope that they do not share a planning time or lunch period with you?

Would they answer any of the above questions "no"? Score one point for each question to which you feel the honest answer would be "no."

These are not easy questions. But after closely examining these questions, do you feel like difficult teachers would answer "no" to at least one of these questions? If the teacher's total score is one or more, then using peer pressure might be effective. If the total is zero, then give one more quiz a chance. Again, ask yourself what the teacher's truthful inner response would be to these multiple choice items. Again ignore public persona.

- Do you hope that your peers: (a) respect you, or (b) disrespect you?

- Do you hope that your peers: (a) feel you are an effective teacher, or (b) feel that you are an ineffective teacher?

- Do you hope that your peers: (a) hold you in high regard, or (b) do not hold you in high regard?

- Do you hope that your peers: (a) like you, or (b) do not like you?

If the difficult teachers you were thinking of would be truthful to themselves and answer any of the above questions with an "a" then using their peers might be beneficial. There may be some extremely rare teachers who might answer "b" to each question above. With these individuals, we will try a different approach. Be aware that for this method to be effective, the difficult teachers do not have to hope that *all* of their peers would like and respect them. It can work even if they hope that only a couple of peers would like and respect them.

This approach is also not for the weak of stomach. It is also never to be taken lightly. I generally see it as appropriate only after trying many other methodologies. When you have a person who is truly difficult, however, this approach may have a positive impact.

I would like to share a couple of examples of using peers to help effect an emotional change in your difficult staff member. I have worked with many schools that are making the transition from the junior-high to the middle-school concept. One facet of this is establishing interdisciplinary teams. An interdisciplinary team might include four teachers; one each in math, science, social studies, and language arts. They work together with a group of approximately 100 students. Typically, the principal determines these teams with input from the teachers.

An appropriate method for gathering teacher input is to privately meet with teachers and inquire with whom they would most like to work. The principal should also ask whether there are any teachers with whom they would feel particularly uncomfortable. In most schools, the names of the difficult teachers come up repeatedly when the individual staff members share with whom they would least want to work. This peer information should compel a principal to have a conversation with the difficult teacher(s). But rather than just use this to humiliate or beat down the less effective staff members, it should be used to provide specific direction and growth opportunities for these difficulty faculty. Here is an example.

I was responsible for opening a new middle school, to which I was adding several staff members because of interdisciplinary teaming. We were hiring some teachers who were new to the district and recruiting some teachers who had requested transfers from other schools. One teacher who was transferring in had a very poor reputation. She was known as someone who yelled at students, used cutting sarcasm, put down students, had a short temper, and who was a negative influence on the school climate. I knew I was going to "inherit" this person; that was a given. However, I asked the superintendent whether I could interview her prior to the time she received official notification of her transfer. The superintendent allowed this with the understanding that no matter how the session went she was coming to my school. I also was aware that she liked to display open disdain for administrators. This did not concern me personally, but it was an important factor in considering the approach of using peer perspectives. Someone who has little regard for the perspective of a principal may care a great deal about the feelings of peers.

I met with this difficult teacher privately a few days later. After some small talk, I asked her in a very calm, relaxed, and caring manner, "Do you hope that the teachers in this school will like you?" As you can imagine, this raised her discomfort level greatly. She hesitated, stammered, and then inquired, "Why do you ask?"

In a very concerned, soft manner, I shared several truths. I stated, "The reason I asked is because many of the teachers who will be at the school shared their concern about working with you. Numerous teachers stated that they did not care who they worked with as long as they did not work with you."

She showed a visible emotional reaction. Not of anger, but of sadness. I then asked her again, in a very sympathetic manner, if she hoped that the people she was going to be working with would like and respect her. When she responded affirmatively, I went into specific detail regarding what that might entail on her part.

I very calmly and sensitively shared with this person, "I have heard, and so have many of the faculty here, many stories about the approach you sometimes take with students. It may not have any truth to it. But, regardless, if people have a perception of something then it oftentimes becomes true. The staff and I have heard several troubling things about your interactions with students. One of the most worrisome is that you yell at students. We do not do that here at our school. They have also indicated you have a reputation for losing your temper, belittling students, using sarcasm, etc."

And softly I noted that, "We always treat our students with respect in this school and these are approaches that I, and the staff, believe in strongly. However, one of the things that we expect as a school is that each year all students have a chance to be successful regardless of their background, reputation, or history. I expect everyone here to apply that same standard to any new staff members."

This conversation was always gentle in tone. Yet, it was very direct. This difficult teacher was not used to dealing with things in an open, emotional sharing way so this was very uncomfortable for her. However, she shared that she wanted to be respected by her coworkers. She added she understood that the standards we had for the way we treated our students would be the major determinant of how she would be received by the other teachers in the school. This was quite an emotional confession on her part.

This approach of opening an emotional avenue by utilizing a difficult teacher's regard for her peers provided a very teachable moment. It also provided an avenue for setting my guidelines and expectations for staff approach to students. She understood clearly that at our school we do not yell at students, use sarcasm, belittle the children we work with, etc. I am very confident that being able to get her to become emotional set the standard for our relationship. Her discomfort with being emotional, combined with her hope for peer approval, set a very positive tone for her teaching performance in our school. Interestingly, once this emotional path was opened it was one that I could use effectively in the future to help remind her of the expectations regarding her approach and treatment of students.

Whenever I was in the halls or during my frequent informal visits to her classroom, I would be very sensitive to her approach toward the children in her class. If she ever became slightly inappropriately aggressive toward the students or even had a hint of sarcasm in her tone, I would calmly whisper—in the same tone and manner that I used in our first interview conversation, "That tone that I just heard, that is what I was talking about. We do not deal with students in that manner here at our school." This was a powerful reminder for the increasingly less difficult staff member. I needed to use this tone and approach less and less frequently because of the impact of the discussion involving her peers.

Because of the close correlation between difficult teachers and feelings of low self-worth, being able to reach them on an emotional level can be of great value. This is particularly true if the staff member tends to be "left-brained" by nature. In other words, if proof, facts, or logical arguments are important to that staff member, then the principal should avoid the "reasoning" approach that the staff member is most comfortable with. Appealing to emotion may be the most effective way to impact this person. A very effective way to do so is by utilizing peer pressure.

A second example again involves a very challenging and difficult staff member. This person would regularly make inappropriate, hurtful, or sarcastic comments to students. But, like a lot of difficult staff members, there was always an excuse at the ready. He was always, "just kidding," and after these discussions he would discontinue the behaviors for a limited time. This teacher was also just capable enough that when the pressure was on regarding classroom performance, he would consistently achieve a minimally acceptable level. So dismissal was probably not a realistic option. Instead, if this individual would stop the inappropriate remarks and put forth just a little bit more effort, he would progress from the difficult category. Additionally, this teacher was just smart enough to be surreptitious in his efforts. He would also consistently make attempts to turn conversations regarding improvement into personal arguments or battles. They did not result in any kind of substantial alteration.

This person seemed to be incredibly unhappy as evidenced by the way he carried himself, approached work, and especially by his approach to life. One day when he was in the hallway I asked him, again in a caring and gentle tone, "Are you okay? The reason I ask is because a couple of other teachers asked me, 'Is Mr. Johnson doing all right? He seems so unhappy. Several of the students told us about some very inappropriate comments he had made in his classes.'" The fact that other teachers were aware of his problems was very disconcerting to him. This approach also reinforced, in a powerful way, what things he was doing that were inappropriate. The fact that other teachers thought they were wrong often carried much more influence than if the principal felt that they were improper. He appeared to be upset and very uncomfortable. More importantly, his approach to his classes improved. He did not seem to have much concern for what the students thought of him and he probably did not have a great level of concern for his principal's perception, but his anonymous coworkers' comments made him uneasy enough to alter his approach.

Although not using peers directly, similar approaches with logical, difficult teachers can also be effective. In the same relaxed, concerned manner described previously ask a disgruntled teacher, "Are you okay? The reason I was asking is because I heard you yelling at the students." This can be an effective approach in making the difficult teacher uncomfortable.

Recall the teacher whom parents imitated at an open house. I calmly shared with this teacher the following: "I happened to see a couple of parents in the hallway acting like they were very angry. They had their hands on their hips and were making very exaggerated gestures. I assumed they were really upset. Then I realized, they were imitating you." Then with great concern and compassion I would add, "I am telling you this because I would want to know." The level of discomfort is much higher and people feel much less argumentative, if you can share observations through someone else's eyes. This is doubly true if you have previously attempted to communicate your personal perspective with few positive results.

A parallel exists, if there is a teacher with a bad temper. You can sometimes continually try to assist, encourage, and at some point offer suggestions regarding maintaining an even temper. However, if this is a difficult teacher and these approaches are ineffective, then a more emotional approach may be effective. Gently and yet directly sharing a story about how you observed several students in the cafeteria all imitating the teacher's behaviors and then making fun of their actions is a powerful persuader. Again, adding the comment, "I am just sharing this with you, because I would want to know" is an approach that is helpful even though the approach itself may seem very aggressive.

The truth is that if you had a mannerism that was very inappropriate and offensive to people, you would want to know. Think about your best teachers. If they were doing things that were inappropriate and hurting students or parents, they would want to know. So do not feel the need to avoid sharing this information with your challenging faculty. This is also an example of what I cover in the next chapter: always assume that they want to do what is right.

# 9

# Always Assume That They Want To Do What Is Right

Expectations for difficult staff members are often very low. You often get what you expect. If expectations do not change, then it is illogical to think that results will. This is why it is critical always to assume that difficult teachers want to do what is right. This is just as appropriate for all of our staff. Always maintaining high expectations can help raise the morale and climate of any school.

There is an old story about a new sixth grade teacher in a K–6 elementary school. Although this was her first year teaching, the principal gave Miss Brown the toughest class in the school. Not only was it the most difficult group of sixth graders this year, it was the most challenging group ever in the school. Every staff member knew this was the most challenging group in the school because they had had them previously. All teachers knew except, of course, Miss Brown.

Like all new teachers she was extremely excited about her first day of teaching. She had spent years looking forward to having a great and positive impact on children. However, after 30 minutes into her first day, she could not believe the students! They were the worst behaved students she had ever seen, and it went downhill from there. The students were the last to line up at recess, the most noisy in the hallways, and the most disrespectful students in the school. By the end of the day, Miss Brown had decided she was going to quit education.

However, after thinking about it over night and contemplating her student loans, Miss Brown decided to give it one more chance. Hoping to develop some idea regarding what to do, Miss Brown went in early and examined all of her students' permanent records. What she discovered amazed her. She could not believe her eyes. Her students IQ scores were exceptional. They were 134, 143, 129, 152, etc. So Miss Brown developed a plan.

That day, when her students first arrived, she told them the news. Miss Brown shared with her students, "I arrived early today because I was so frustrated with class yesterday. I went to the office and looked up your permanent records. I saw your IQ scores and discovered that this is a gifted class. Since we are a gifted class we are going to change our behavior. We are going to be the first to line up at recess, the quietest class in the hallways, and the most respectful students in the school."

The amazing thing was, it started to happen. The children in Miss Brown's class became the most well behaved, polite, and respectful students in the school. All of the other teachers were shocked. They would walk by this well-behaved group of students that every year had been the loudest, most obnoxious class in the school, and they were stunned. Even the principal could not understand. Finally he sat down with Miss Brown and asked her, "What is going on? These students used to be the most disrespectful students in the school and now they are the most polite."

Miss Brown shared her tale of how terrible the students were the first day of school. She described to the principal how she was so frustrated that she was going to quit. She went on to explain how she came in early, examined their permanent records, and saw their IQ scores of 134, 143, 129, 152, etc.; how she shared with the class that they are a gifted group and that their behavior should be exemplary; and how their behavior changed.

The principal asked Miss Brown to show him what records she examined. They went down to the office and she opened up her students' permanent records and she showed him the IQ scores of 134, 143, 129, 152, etc. The principal fought off a smile and said, "Miss Brown, I do not want to burst your bubble, but these are the students' locker numbers."

Well this fictitious tale involving students has the same application to working with staff members. Treating all teachers as though they want to do what is right can have positive effects on everyone, including difficult teachers. Let us examine a typical situation in a school. In schools that have bells and passing times, principals often hope that teachers supervise the hallways between classes. However, as people become busy or simply disinclined to supervise, the number of teachers monitoring hallways drops unacceptably. A typical approach to getting more teachers in the hallway is to write a memo or make an announcement at the next faculty meeting. This approach often includes language such as, "A responsibility of every teacher in the school is to supervise the hallways between each class! It is important that everyone be in the hall during passing time. I know that some of you are not. It is in the teachers' handbook, so between every class you should be supervising." Just how effective is this approach?

Recall the three questions we described earlier in the book regarding whether we should implement a new rule:

1.  What is my *true* purpose in implementing this rule or policy?

2.  Will it actually accomplish this purpose?

3.  How will my most positive and productive people feel about this policy?

Let us use these same three questions to examine how effective this approach would be in enforcing a policy. The goal of the principal is to have more teachers supervise the hallways. Assume this issue is being addressed at a staff meeting and we will think through the effect of this approach.

Given that a staff consists of superstars, backbones, and mediocres, which of these groups is most likely already supervising the hallways? The superstars. Which of these groups are least likely to be supervising the hallways? The mediocres. Which of these groups is most important? The superstars. At table A is a group of mediocres. At table B is a group of superstars. The principal offers the following monologue to the entire staff.

"You teachers need to be in the hallways between classes! It is in the handbook and it is an expectation for everyone in this school. Two kids got in a fight today because no one was in the hallway. I expect each of you there everyday!"

Now remember, the goal is to get teachers to be in the hallway more. After this lecture, how do the mediocres feel? They probably feel indifferent or mad. Perhaps they were not even paying attention. The question is, are they more likely to be in the hallway tomorrow? Probably not.

After this lecture how do the superstars, who have been in the halls between classes, feel? They may wonder why you are talking to them. They might feel frustrated and angry. Are they more or less likely to be in the hallway tomorrow? Probably not more and even if they are, they might be disgruntled about it.

Now we will rewind and start the faculty meeting over. At table A is a group of mediocres. At table B is a group of superstars. The principal gives the following monologue to the entire staff.

In a sincere and gentle tone, the principal says, "I know how busy each of you is here at school. Everyone's plate is so full. But I want to take a minute out and thank those of you who take that extra effort to step out and supervise the hallways between each class. I know your time is precious. However, it does make a big difference. Today I happened to be in a hallway in which two students were about to fight. One of them noticed a teacher nearby. I don't even think the teacher saw them. The student who saw the teacher pointed her out to the potential combatant. They then went their separate ways. I sincerely want to thank each of you who take that extra effort to help make our school a safer place. It is much appreciated."

After this lecture, how do the mediocres feel? Perhaps they feel guilty; they might wish they were receiving the attention. Perhaps they are indifferent. Many of them would feel pretty uncomfortable. Are they more or less likely to be in the hallway tomorrow? Some are more likely to be in the hallway. But remember, these are your least important people.

After this lecture how do the superstars, who have been in the halls between classes, feel? They are likely to feel proud, valued, and appreciated. Are they more or less likely to be in the hallway tomorrow? They are much more likely to help supervise the hallways. Keep in mind that we continually make decisions based on how our positive faculty will receive them.

Here is another example of how treating people *as though* they were doing what is right may be more powerful than treating them *as is*. We are all familiar with disciplinary referrals where students are written up and sent to the office for negative offenses. One of the programs I implemented as an administrator was a positive referral program. Teachers would write a student a positive referral for something good and put it in my mailbox. They could write a positive referral because a student received a good grade on a test, because the teacher enjoyed seeing the student's smiling face every day, or because the teacher saw the student assist someone in need.

I would call the student to my office and share the good news. I would also pick up the phone and call a parent or guardian to share this positive message. If at all possible, I would contact this parent or guardian at work. The busier the office or the more crowded the assembly line the better the call. When I first initiated these calls I would say, "This is Todd Whitaker, principal at Middle Grove Junior High School." Before I could continue I would often hear a loud moan of, "Oh, no!" at the other end of the line. Then I would go on the say, "I hate to bother you at work, but I just thought you might want to know that a teacher, Mr. Green, is running around at this school bragging on your son. He shared with me that Johnny got a B+ on his math quiz . . ." etc.

The most common response I heard parents say was that no

school has ever called with anything good before. This was the most frequent comment regardless of whether it was a parent of a student who had been in trouble several times or of the future valedictorian of the school. This helped me to understand why people may tend to believe the bad things they read or hear about education. If they have never heard good things, then what else are they supposed to believe?

I always tried to contact a parent at work because I realized that many parents, after drawing such attention to themselves with their initial shout of, "Oh, no!" would immediately brag to everyone that the principal from Middle Grove Junior High School just called them with some good news. I realized that having people say good things about you and your school is a pretty beneficial occurrence. It also had a positive effect on the student. Many students shared that their parents were so proud of them that they made a special effort at home to reinforce their positive behavior. The positive referrals also resulted in very positive relations between the students and myself.

Our school received such positive attention from this program that we decided to expand the concept the next year. Each teacher would make one positive phone call a week. When we first decided to begin this process, I realized that if teachers had not initiated positive contact with parents in their careers then the only contact they may have ever had was negative. Because of this, many of my faculty were fearful and uncomfortable in contacting parents. We had several meetings regarding how to make positive calls and contacts and I role-played several of the approaches that I had used the previous year.

As you can imagine, the superstars and many of the backbones began the process and had wonderful feedback from the parents they contacted. They also received many accolades from the students in their classes because of the praise they received at home from the parents. However, I also knew that some of the difficult teachers would resist making these calls as long as possible. Knowing that making difficult teachers uncomfortable is often a step to change, I decided to attempt a new approach at the next staff meeting.

Our faculty meetings were on Wednesday after school. So

on Wednesday morning before school, I was making my usual rounds and stopped by one of my superstar teachers, Mrs. Meyers, and informally asked her whether she had had the opportunity to make a positive phone call yet. She responded cheerfully, "Yes!" I asked her to tell me about it and she gladly did. I then asked Mrs. Meyers whether she would mind sharing this at the staff meeting this afternoon and she indicated she would be happy to do so.

I then went by another superstar's room, Mr. Mitchell. I asked him the same question, and he had shared that he had called a parent the day before, and they were so pleased. Again, I asked whether he would mind sharing his story at this afternoon's meeting. He expressed he would be glad to do so.

It is also important to note that if either of the superstars had not reached a parent yet, I would not have reprimanded them. Instead I would have been very supportive and said it was okay. I would have added that I would very much like to hear about the call when they had the opportunity to call in the future.

At the end of the faculty meeting, I said, "One last thing; has anyone had a chance to contact any parents regarding our positive phone call program yet?" Mr. Mitchell raised his hand. I called on this volunteer and he shared with the staff what he had done and how well it went. I thanked him for his efforts and asked whether anyone else had made a positive phone call. Mrs. Meyers indicated that she had and that the call was very well received.

I said how much I appreciated their calls and what a difference it makes for all of us to be viewed in a positive light by our students, parents, and community. I then looked around the room and politely asked one of the most difficult teachers in the school who was desperately avoiding eye contact, "How did your positive phone call go . . . Mrs. Grubb?"

A quick question: Who was the most uncomfortable person in the room? My most difficult teacher, Mrs. Grubb, of course. Who were the next most uncomfortable people in the room? All of the others who had not made the phone calls.

Mrs. Grubb, being very argumentative by nature, gruffly responded, "I did not make a positive phone call. I was too busy

dealing with my fifth-hour class. You know how rude they are."
I politely, respectfully, and with a friendly smile said, "I understand. I know how busy everybody is. How about if we start off
next month's meeting with your call." Not only was Mrs. Grubb
uncomfortable at that moment, but now she had the chance to
be worried for an entire month!

If we treat people as though they are doing things right, then
we can approach everyone in the same manner.

This approach is critical in working with the most difficult
staff members. If you asked them in an accusatory manner, "I
assume you haven't started working on that project yet have
you?" they will immediately put up their all too familiar barriers. They have great practice with this mind-set and are quite at
home with this approach. An argumentative relationship has
been established and there is no incentive to be more productive. If, by some chance, they have begun working on it, then
you are in the uncomfortable position rather than the teacher.

Approaching those same teachers with a professional "How
is everything going on the project?" causes them to feel much
greater discomfort, if they have not progressed on it. More importantly, if they have, there is a positive foundation for enhanced
relations. The expectation of assuming that the difficult teachers want to do what is right can increase their discomfort without damaging relations with either the challenging staff members
or the more positive teachers.

# Part 4

# Communicating with the Difficult Teacher

# 10

# Approach Them When You Are Ready

One challenge we face in working with difficult teachers is knowing specifically how and when to address them about their inappropriate actions. Being able to choose the most opportune and effective time is essential. If we do not handle the initial contact in an appropriate manner, we potentially escalate the situation and it can even become a school-wide issue. There is good news and bad news about choosing when to communicate with ineffective staff members about their actions. The good news is that if we miss an opportunity today, there will probably be another one tomorrow. The bad news is that if we miss an opportunity today, there will probably be another one tomorrow. Many of our less valued teachers' inappropriate behaviors regularly recur. However, do not feel the need to rush or to immediately address them regarding the issue. Often, they have repeated their behaviors for years. Though this does not make it right, it does mean that whatever they have been doing has not caused the school to close. Yet, it is also important to work to prevent it from happening again as soon as possible. Understand that it is essential that *you* feel comfortable before you choose to approach teachers regarding their behavior. The more comfortable you feel, the more likely it is that they will feel uncomfortable. The opposite is also true. The less prepared you are to interact with them, the more likely they are to feel empowered in the conversation. Let's take a look at a scenario we previously discussed in the book and think through how to choose the best time to approach a staff member.

## First, Determine When You Are Comfortable

One of the challenges we face is that when teachers do something that they should not, we often feel very emotional about their behavior. And we should. If a student is treated inappropriately, this should be very troublesome to us. This touches our emotions and causes a reaction within us. It may be discomfort, it may be anger, and it may be hurt. All of these are appropriate. But our main goal is not to "take it out" on the teacher. It is important to not lose sight of our main goal, which is to have the teacher behave differently. We have to be prepared with a strategy prior to interacting with the difficult teacher.

## When Will They Be Most Uncomfortable?

Even the most difficult teachers, at times, become aware that they crossed the line of appropriateness. When this happens, they become uncomfortable. During the time immediately following their misdeed, they may be on their best behavior for a while. The reason is simple. They are uncomfortable for a brief time. Additionally, if they really do feel like their actions were wrong, they may even seek you out to try to get it resolved. They want this situation settled so they can feel more comfortable again. When they feel that they are on more stable ground, they are likely to revert to their previous negative ways.

If at all possible, do not be in a hurry to interact with the teacher. There is a chance that your emotions will be high and you might not be in control of yourself. It is much easier to get caught up in an argument or lose track of the real purpose of your confrontation, which is the teacher's inappropriate behavior. Instead, gather your thoughts and have a specific game plan before meeting with the teacher. If you happen to run into this person or if the teacher requests to meet with you, I would encourage you to delay the meeting if you are not prepared. As busy as you are, it is not too difficult to generate a reason why you cannot talk with the teacher at this time. If you feel that the teacher is not aware that you know of the offending occurrence, then you have no obligation to address it immediately. I would not even commit to a time. The more it is unknown the less comfortable the teacher may be. This compares to a child waiting until dad got home from work to receive punishment. Often the most grueling part was the waiting.

Let's refocus on an example from Chapter 7 regarding the counselor who was behaving improperly when having a meeting with a student and a parent. You recall that the counselor was leaning back in his chair, yawning, and looking at his watch while interacting with these nice people. Instinctively we might believe that immediately addressing him would be best. However, our adrenaline may lead us to approach that interaction in a less effective manner. We need to have a chance to gather our thoughts. Additionally, we can wait several days or even longer before we visit with someone about an offensive behavior. In this situation, the counselor may not have even been aware of what he was doing. Whether he was or not, we are going to inform him that his actions were unacceptable. We are not doing it to hurt or embarrass him. We want to cause a change in his behavior.

It is also important to determine the best place to visit with offending staff. Our first thoughts may be to place a note in their mailbox telling them that we need to see them in our office. Realize though that with our most challenging staff members any time they have advance notice, they get mentally prepared with an excuse for anything they have ever done wrong in their entire lives. The more notice they have, the more comfortable they become. One of their methods of making themselves comfortable could be to put on their emotional shield. Maybe it will involve excuses regarding their personal life. If they have any forewarning, they will have prepared a way to feel more comfortable.

Instead, we need to be the ones who are prepared. We should also plan so that they will not be. I actually waited a day before I had a conversation with the counselor. In between, I treated

him in the professional manner that I always did. I wanted him
to have his guard down. The less prepared he was the more
uncomfortable he would become.

The next day when I went in, sat down, and gently shared
with the counselor that I was offended when I saw him leaning
back in his chair, yawning, and looking at his watch, he was
very uncomfortable. If, instead of the delay, I had immediately
followed up his conference with the parent and student by going in and addressing his behavior, he would have been much
more equipped to respond. Anything from, "They had been in
here so long," or "I see them all the time" could be his potential
responses. Of course, he could raise these or other excuses at
any future point also. But the less ready he is, the more uncomfortable he is likely to be.

## The Broken Record

In this same situation, what if the counselor raises an excuse? After all, our most troubling teachers may have spent years
making them up. Well if he does, respond with a broken record.
Just repeat what you originally said. "I was offended when I
saw you lean back in your chair, look at your watch, and yawn."
Do not feel the need to respond to his excuses. Difficult people
are very skilled at deflecting the attention from their behavior
to someone else's actions. He may question why you care or
how annoying those people were. But it is essential that you not
lose sight of the issue. The issue is his behavior, not yours, the
student's, or the parent's. If he continues to shift the conversation away from his actions to others, you can continue to repeat
your record, "I was offended when I saw you lean back in your
chair, look at your watch, and yawn."

If this seems that it could go on in perpetuity, feel free to
conclude it by gently sharing that you were just telling him because, "I would want you to know." By repeating his behaviors
and deflecting attention back to him, you will maintain control
of the discussion. After you share that you would want him to
know, feel free to exit slowly and repeat that you were just telling him, "because I would want you to know."

This same approach is effective if Jim would want to bring in representatives from the teachers' association. If they challenge your actions, you could sincerely ask the union officials if they would feel more comfortable if you documented his behavior. I have great faith that they would rather not have you put pen to paper. You could also ask gently and politely if they would want to know if they were behaving in a way that was offfensive to others. It is very difficult to respond in the negative and you also continue to reinforce that you were doing this as a way to support the teacher. After all, if the best teacher would want to know, shouldn't we treat everyone equally?

# 11

# The Best Teacher, Worst Teacher Test

How can we know if the communications with our most challenging staff members are appropriate? Because our superstars and other quality staff members are our most essential teachers, how can we feel assured that they are comfortable with our interactions with their less effective peers? We need to have self-checks that can help us feel more confident regarding our approach with some of our most troubling teachers.

## Always Approach the Teacher as if the Whole Staff Were in the Room

Your effective teachers want you to work toward improving the difficult and negative members of the staff. They may even want you to eliminate them from the building. However, the rest of the staff wants and expects you to deal with the difficult teacher in a professional and appropriate manner. Following this guideline can help prevent backlash from your effective staff members. Always think, "Could I do this if some of my best teachers were observing?" and if the answer is yes, then you are probably acting appropriately.

Visualizing the thoughts of the entire group can be very beneficial. It can also be quite challenging and complex to attempt.

Rather than trying to predict the reactions of your whole faculty, let's center on a more precise scenario.

## The Best Teacher, Worst Teacher Test

A principal can also develop a more specific standard to follow. As we are well aware, many of our most challenging staff members are continually in the gossip and rumor mill mode. Whenever anything occurs that they feel might incite others, they often want to be the first bearers of bad news. This is also true when we directly address our most reluctant staff members. We have to continually assess the staff members' reactions to our approach. Since one of our goals is to make them uncomfortable, we are trying to elicit a reaction. If this discomfort does not manifest itself, then most likely neither will the impending change.

Yet more essential than the less effective teachers' reactions is the potential response of others in the school. Let's narrow down the list of potential responders to two.

Imagine that whenever you communicate with your weakest staff members they are going to follow up your conversation with one of their own. Only their conversation will not be with you. Instead, their first thought is to scurry to the teachers' workroom and share what happened with whoever is in there. Unfortunately, it probably does not take a great deal of imagination to think troubled teachers are going to look for an empathetic ear to share their woes after you have placed responsibility for their behavior where it belongs—on them. However, you are going to visualize two specific staff members in the workroom every time a challenging staff member goes in. Imagine that this troubled educator's audience will always be with the same two teachers. The most effective teacher in the school and the least effective teacher in the school will be there and hear this teacher's regurgitation of your conversation. (If your conversation was actually with the least effective teacher, feel free to substitute the second worst!) Do not be concerned about how close to the facts this teacher will be. Everyone has his or her own view and good people are quite aware of the tendency to taint the story to one's advantage. Instead of picturing what this teacher is saying, focus on the reactions of the two audience members. How would they react?

If you handled it appropriately, you should readily be able to predict their reactions. If Jim, the counselor, shares his woes about you discussing his leaning back in his chair, yawning, and looking at his watch, what would the reactions of his equals be?

The best teacher will seem very concerned and reflective to the troubled teacher talking — that is on the exterior. But internally the good teacher is ready to hug you. Finally, a principal is attempting to confront this teacher. For twenty-three years this teacher has behaved in this manner and for the first time someone is addressing it. Get ready for an emotional high five when you see that staff member.

Realize they have to show empathy to their cohort. There is nothing wrong with that. You need and want them to maintain their respect level with all staff members. If any of the teachers lose respect for your superstars, then these leaders' ability to influence others will be diminished. The best teachers' outward reaction is not important. Their inward thoughts and emotions are the essential components. If they would be pleased with the way you approached this teacher, then this is a very valuable stamp of approval.

Our best teachers would love it if we could "fix" their most challenging colleagues. Who wouldn't? But what they more reasonably expect is for you to try. They know how difficult this peer is. After all, they may have worked with this person longer than you have. They do not expect an overnight miracle. However, they do expect and deserve to have you attempt to impact their peer. It is very similar to a classroom situation involving a misbehaving student. The other students want the teacher to intervene and attempt to corral the inappropriate actions of the classmate. Yet they are often aware that this student has behaved in this manner for years. They do not specifically expect the teacher to "fix" the student. They know how troubled this student is because they have been classmates for years. And though they can accept that the teacher may not be able to prevent the rude actions entirely, they can and do expect their teacher to try in a professional and appropriate manner to positively impact their fellow pupil.

This is the same thing that our positive teachers desire. They insist on and deserve a professional effort to intervene and diminish the actions of their more negative peers. If they see a genuine effort, their acceptance of us is likely to continually increase as long as they view it as appropriate.

We can probably predict the mental reaction of the positive teacher in the workroom. What about their less effective workroom fellows? How might they be reacting?

Externally they could easily be feeding the negative energies of the report shared by the teacher that just left the conversation. They could be aggressively reassuring them how wronged they were. They need to do this to maintain the "griper bond" that they have built over the years. But let's examine what they are feeling and thinking inside.

The teachers will likely become reflective and worried. They might externally share how inappropriate the principal was. They have to maintain this leathery interior. But internally they could be reflecting, "I wonder whether I ever lean back in my chair, yawn, or look at my watch at inappropriate times." When this happens, you will not have to have the same conversation with them. Instead, they are more likely to judiciously eliminate these offensive actions independent of you. Even if they do not, just ask yourself which of these two teachers in the "audience" is most comfortable and which is least comfortable. What does my best teacher think of my efforts? How is the less effective staff member feeling? By having this mental two-person test, it can enable us to self-check our approaches before we pursue them.

## Sharing with Peers Makes Your Job Easier

There is nothing enjoyable about communicating with weaker staff members about their behaviors. We would all rather not do it. One of the benefits of approaching the whole faculty in a positive manner is to reduce the number of small group conversations we may need to have. In Chapter 9 we use the example of increasing the number of teachers who would be supervising the hallway between classes. By focusing on those who are in the halls, instead of those who are not, we take a more positive approach to increasing supervision. If you still feel the need to address individuals, that is up to you. However, if I do feel the need to converse with teachers who are not supervising, I would like it to be as small a number as possible. If we effectively converse with one teacher about being irresponsible, potentially this teacher will be our messenger to others. If we do so appropriately and professionally, one staff member can carry the warning flag to the rest of the staff. This could also help determine which person to address individually first. You might be tempted to start with the individual who would conform quickest. This could be a starting point. You might also consider who will run and tell the largest number of others so that you will have fewer offenders to interact with.

## One to One, Not One to All

We never should address the inappropriate actions of one to an entire group. In a faculty meeting, if we say to our staff, "Some of you have been arriving at school late," two things result. One is that the teachers who are prompt resent being lectured regarding this issue. The other is that we allow the offenders to hide. They could easily not be attentive or even not in attendance at the meeting. If they did hear and are aware that they are not appropriately prompt, we still take the pressure off of them. They are likely to think, "Oh good, there must be quite a few of us who are late. That is why she is addressing the entire faculty." This allows the tardy teachers to be more comfortable than if we have a private individual conversation.

If we mention this as an expectation at the start of the year, it is a different mind-set. If at staff meetings at the beginning of the year we say how much we value professionalism and include actions such as dress, promptness, etc., we are then addressing expectations of the future. This is not the same level of offensiveness in tone. No one should feel defensive because no one has done any of these things yet as the year has not yet started.

One of the excuses sometimes given for hesitancy in having one-on-one conversations with teachers regarding their inappropriate behaviors is that we do not want to hurt their feelings. Though there could be some sprinkle of truth in this, a more realistic reason is that we do not want to hurt our *own* feelings. Often our biggest concern is how we will feel if someone we are having a discussion with gets angry or cries. As caring and concerned people, we do react to these things. There is nothing wrong with reacting to someone's emotional actions. It is probably impossible not to react. But as a leader, you cannot allow this to prevent you from doing what is needed and what is right. It is okay to look out for yourself. Potentially you are the only one doing so. But it is mandatory that you look out for your students' best interests.

# 12

# Focus on Eliminating Behaviors

We all wish that every teacher in our school put the needs of students first. Every school has many staff members that readily do so, and some schools have others that are a little more reticent to put the student needs front and center. Potentially a few staff members' actions may seem a little more self-centered than student-centered. One challenge all leaders face is to change the beliefs or feelings of their staff. This is quite a noble effort, and I would encourage everyone to work at doing so. One of the limitations we face in doing this is that we cannot know what someone's true internal convictions are. The only thing we can really measure are their actions. These actions may or may not be a result of their sentiments. To the students in our schools and classrooms, the reasons teachers do things are not what they are affected by. What we actually see and are affected by are a person's actions, not beliefs. Let's look at an example involving a very effective teacher.

Teachers in school will always have students that they like more than others. Conversely teachers also have students that they are less drawn to. It does not matter who these teachers are, we all have favorite students and others that do not rank quite as high on our appeal list. This is true of our best, most caring teachers and equally true of staff members who might be on the other end of the productivity spectrum. Now I would agree that your best teachers may have many more students they feel close to than do your less quality employees. Though the quantities may vary, the variations of feelings toward students are consistent. However, what is very different is the way the teachers *treat* their students. The best teachers act with care and concern for every student regardless of how they feel about them. The least effective staff members often have trouble showing any empathy, even toward students that are their favorites.

You might believe that the feelings toward students vary greatly between teachers. I would agree with this. And most likely there is a pretty high correlation between the feelings teachers have toward others and the way they treat them But it is irrefutable that the behaviors toward students are dramatically different among our staff members. The students see this differing behavior among teachers immediately. Our very best teachers treat all of the students with respect no matter how they feel about them.

As leaders, we have to make sure that we continually center on eliminating teachers' negative behaviors from the school. It is easy to be drawn in a differing direction. When we are communicating with our most troubled teachers, they will work very hard at deflecting our efforts away from their behaviors. They will want the attention to be about someone or something else. By keeping your focus on the teacher's actions, it is easier to bring about improvement.

## Defending Ineffective Teachers

There is nothing that causes me to bristle more than hearing a principal defend an ineffective teacher. Because of my writing and presenting, I interact with numerous principals on a regular basis. Many times I receive questions regarding unsettling staff members in a school. Amazingly, after describing some totally inappropriate behavior, the next sentence often is, "But they are good teachers." The offending teachers may use obscene language to students. The principals might share that "They are good teachers, they just have trouble getting along with the students." It might involve bad-tempered staff members who severely overreact several times during the year.

When we really reflect on this, seldom are these employees good teachers. They may not be the worst teachers in a district. They may have abilities in some areas. They may be intelligent and know their subject. But generally when people have repetitive inappropriate behaviors, seldom are they *good* teachers.

A good standard of comparison is to ask yourself, "How many years would one of my excellent teachers have to teach to exhibit such behavior?" If the answer is they would never do that, then the offending teachers are probably not "good" teachers. This does not mean at all that they should be attacked. It does not even mean that they need to be labeled. Instead, the hope is that we stop being so quick to defend. Principals do it, superintendents do it, and so do other teachers. We never would intentionally humiliate or hurt anyone in our organization. However, by defending ineffective teachers, we potentially reinforce their behaviors and encourage others to defend and emulate them.

## But, My Personal Life . . .

One defense that many ineffective employees use relates to their personal life. "I yelled at the student because of my marriage." Or "I humiliated a child because of concern about my daughter." Effective principals have almost unlimited empathy and understanding regarding the personal concerns of their staff members. Yet when we examine more closely, we realize that everyone faces personal demands when away from school and these things ebb and flow for each teacher. However, our most effective teachers seldom, if ever, allow these things to affect the way they treat the students. This does not mean that we should not be sensitive to the personal problems our teachers face. It is essential that we do show compassion when necessary. But we also need to be aware that these outside influences cannot consistently be used as an excuse for adults behaving inappropriately in our schools.

Realize that we do not even allow this behavior by our students. Just because a student is in a bad mood does not give the child freedom to hit others. This does not mean that we would not try to cut a little wider swath for our students, because we do. However, there are still limits on unacceptable behaviors.

The best approach is to analyze whether the teacher's behavior changes are temporary. If the teacher is having a bad day and makes students aware of it, they will tolerate it. Students are very understanding if we are not at our best because of something that happened to a family member, etc. However, difficult people continually have excuses to support their wrongful actions. They use anything that is out of their control to defend their improper behaviors. Regardless of their reasons, we cannot allow them to continue their unacceptable behavior in the school. Effective teachers filter out personal issues before the students enter their classrooms. By continually expecting appropriate behaviors from all of our teachers we can have a consistent standard for all. If many of our teachers are able to avoid bringing personal issues with them to school then we can expect this of all staff members.

## Ignorance or Insubordination

When we work with a difficult teacher we have a variety of emotions. We may feel anger, pity, fear, or aggression. A good leader takes everything personally. That is one of the things that makes a leader effective. But when working with lesser quality teachers, we must determine if what they are doing is intentional or because they do not know any better. This same question must be answered when reflecting on student behavior. Did the child unintentionally lose the pencil or did not bring one to class to avoid doing the work? Though we cannot always answer this question, when we can, it takes some of the guilt or pressure off in determining which action to take with the student. This same issue is true with adults.

As a general rule, people use the very best approach that they know. Every teacher tries to take the most effective approach in managing the classrooms. Each teacher wants the students to behave in the classrooms. Yet at times it is more of a challenge to determine the difference between intentional or unintentional poor behavior.

If a teacher remains seated behind the desk a disproportionate amount of the time, we may be able to guess the reason. It could be because the teacher is "too lazy" to get up. It may be because the teacher is in the middle of a hotly contested solitaire game on the computer. Yet it could also be because the teacher doesn't know any better. The teacher may have student-taught with someone who had a similar style or may be imitating that of a long-time colleague. In order to effect a change, it would be beneficial to determine the reason for this teacher's behavior.

This situation is simple to decipher. What do teachers do when the principal walks into their classroom? Do they continue playing solitaire or do they get out of their chair and monitor student behavior? If they continue with the computer game, they might not be aware that their behavior is improper or inappropriate. If they nervously rise and move among the students, then they did know the difference between what they should have been doing and what they were doing. Thus we gather that they know the difference between right and wrong. They are just choosing to behave inappropriately.

This is one of the reasons we have to be so specific when we work to eliminate inappropriate behaviors from our buildings and classrooms. Why was I so specific with Jim the counselor when I discussed his leaning back in his chair, yawning, and looking at his watch? It was essential for him to know which specific behaviors to eliminate. It would not be fair if I expected him to discontinue doing those things if I had not specifically identified the behaviors he needed to stop doing. How could I possibly expect him, on his own, to be aware that he was offending others? After all, he had been behaving that way his entire life. I feel it is safe to assume that either he had no idea those characteristics were offensive *or* he had no idea that he was doing them. And the reason he was doing them was not even relevant. The issue was that he *was* doing them, not *why*. If I was not specific, then I would feel terribly guilty in expecting him to cease the offending actions in the future, without offering him an explanation. However, since I was so specific, it is now *fair* of me to expect him to stop engaging in inappropriate behavior. Should any of these behaviors occur in the future, it is much more likely that they are intentional.

There is an additional reason we need to continually focus on the recurring behaviors that we want stopped. Earlier, I discussed the concept of the broken record, i.e., continually repeating the same thing when someone attempts to deflect attention away from their actions. What do I need from Jim in order to discontinue the broken record? Your initial reaction may be that I need to have him apologize to me. Well, that might be nice, but it wasn't really me I was concerned about, it was the student and her mom. However, my real focus is not on making amends on past behaviors. (After all, many of the most offensive adults we know have little ability or desire to apologize effectively.) I did not need him to repair his relationship with me. And, though it would be nice, I really do not even need for him to apologize to the student and her parent. What I really need is much more basic. I need for him to *not* do it again. The desire is to have him change his behavior in the future. It would be wonderful if our most offending staff members sent notes of apology to everyone they had hurt over the years. We all know this is not realistic. But it is reasonable to expect these teachers to not repeat these offensive behaviors after you have shared specific examples with them and directly asked them to stop. Clear-cut guidance deserves clear-cut remediation.

Without being specific about what behaviors need to be altered, there is no way to know if the offenders are suffering from ignorance or if they are intentionally being insubordinate. Once we raise their knowledge level about what they are doing and what they need to do differently in the future, we can now determine if their actions are intentional. By clarifying our real goal of eliminating inappropriate behaviors from our school, we are more able to help keep our focus on the end result. When we examine observable behaviors, not internal beliefs, we can then determine when improvements have occurred.

## Focus on Our Own Behaviors

The same standard that we are using with our staff members—centering on behaviors—must apply to ourselves. No administrator wants to deal with demanding people. No principal looks forward to a taxing conversation. The difference is that some principals do address negative teacher behaviors and others do not. All of us have teachers we would rather not interact with. Probably all principals have parents from whom they dread receiving phone calls. The difference is that some principals deal with it while others avoid it. You may not be able to control your feelings, but it is essential that you control your actions.

For example, if you see a teacher humiliate a student you may feel great anger. You may even desire to hurt the teacher's feelings the way the teacher hurt the child's. However, as leaders, we cannot always *immediately* act on these impulses. It may be much more professional and effective to wait until we are more prepared to communicate with this staff member regarding these actions. Escalating a behavior is not the outcome we want. Our goal is to improve behaviors, not imitate them. If we are not able to control our own behavior, it is unfair to expect the students and teachers in our school to have a handle on theirs.

It is perfectly acceptable to feel any emotions you may have. Many schools have teachers that other teachers are intimidated by, uncomfortable around, or afraid of. A great number of schools have teachers that the principal is intimidated by, uncomfortable around, or afraid of. There is nothing wrong with this at all. It is human nature. The challenge is not to avoid *feeling* intimidated, afraid, or uncomfortable. The challenge is to not *act* intimidated, afraid, or uncomfortable. Your feelings are all legitimate and justified. Your job is to put these feelings in perspective. It is essential that your behaviors be focused on your goal of improving the teacher. You cannot allow your angry emotions to dictate your actions. You need to: determine what behavior you want changed; decide when and where to meet with the teacher; develop the strategy you will use; and do what is right for the students of your school.

# 13

# Questioning Strategies

Communicating with negative people is seldom fun—especially if the conversation involves their unprofessional behavior. We dread it and quite often our actions reflect this. These people are very good at controlling the conversation and making *others* feel defensive. Being able to determine effective ways to probe a situation is essential to raising our abilities to communicate with our onerous teachers. The more challenging the situation and the more onerous the staff member, the more important it is for us to have a way to lead the conversation in the needed direction. Let's examine a situation and a universally applicable approach.

## Mrs. Grump

A school had three fifth grade teachers. For whatever reason, one of the teachers, Mrs. Grump, was consistently rude to her grade level colleagues. The other two teachers determinedly attempted to build relations during the two years since Mrs. Grump had transferred into the school. Yet no olive branch offered seemed to bring about a change.

Then one Thursday Mrs. Grump asked her two peers if they would like to bring their students into her class for the last ninety minutes on Friday afternoon. Mrs. Grump was going to show a video to her twenty-five students and she wondered if her colleagues would care to have their students join her. Though they were shocked and did not even feel the video was related to the curriculum, they thought this would be a wonderful chance to reinforce Mrs. Grump for her efforts to connect. They assumed that she must have finally seen the light.

The next afternoon the two teachers quietly escorted their fifty students into Mrs. Grump's classroom. After they had settled in, Mrs. Grump pulled the videotape off her desk and marched up to the television, seemingly to start the tape. Right before she pushed the start button, Mrs. Grump announced loudly, "Since my students were so good this week I have cookies and soda for each of my twenty-five pupils."

As you can imagine, the other two teachers did everything they could to keep their jaws from hitting the floor. And, it took quite an effort on their part to keep them from hitting Mrs. Grump's jaw! The teachers felt that they really had no choice but to have their students sit there and squirm while Mrs. Grump handed treats to each of her students. They got through the movie but you can imagine how irate these two staff members were. The video ended just as classes were dismissed, and the two very upset teachers made a bee line for the principal's office.

The teachers explained to the principal what had happened and wanted their leader to do something. But they also wanted the principal not to tell Mrs. Grump that they "told" on her. Quite a dilemma.

Our first thought could be about the two teachers' behaviors. Shouldn't they confront Mrs. Grump? Though that is a possibility, there is also a chance that they are afraid of her. If Mrs. Grump did not feel she intimidated them, she probably never would have tried such a stunt. Additionally, as a principal, it is wonderful if a staff member stands up to a bully teacher. But what happens when someone stands up to a bully? Sometimes the bully does not quit the behavior, but finds a new victim. However, if a principal effectively corrects the situation, then it will prevent this from occurring again in the school.

Unfortunately the scenario you just read is true. What strategies might best support the principal? Let's work our way through it.

## "Tell Me a Little Bit About . . ."

In situations like this, it is overtly obvious that the teacher's action was intentional. Additionally, the person who conceived the plan felt pretty comfortable and confident in the school—not just in relation to the other two teachers, but most likely also regarding the principal. Some of our most dominant negative personalities can be intimidating. How can we approach them? You need a strategy that puts you in control of the situation.

I would encourage you, if at all possible, to allow some time to pass—several days if possible. In between, continue to treat the teacher in a professional manner. The teacher will be likely to lower her guard regarding the situation. Then one day casually walk by Mrs. Grump's room and greet her in your usual friendly manner, "Hi. Mrs. Grump." Keep on walking and then turn around as if you just remembered something and say, "Mrs. Grump, can you tell me a little bit about showing a video to your class?"

You may be thinking this question is not direct enough or far too open-ended. The reason we want to be so nebulous is to keep the discomfort on the teacher. If the teacher is ineffective, she is working very hard to determine what you know and whether or not to lie. The less detail we provide the more stressful it is for the teacher to determine how to respond.

Your inquiry will leave her with a pretty simple decision. Mrs. Grump has to choose whether to lie or tell the truth. No matter whether or not she replies honestly, you treat her the way we discussed in Chapter 9—as if her intentions were not malicious. In other words, no matter whether she says, "I don't know what you are talking about" or "What video?" or "You mean last Friday?" you do not have to have any emotion in your reaction. Just continue to prompt her.

She is also attempting to determine exactly what you know. She has no idea how much you know about what occurred and, as a result, she has a very high level of discomfort. Your next prompt can delve a little more.

"Mrs. Grump, can you tell me about something to do with a video and some treats?" And you can continue to pry. If she says, "I don't know anything about a video and treats," pretend as if she is telling the truth. You can say something like, "Okay, thanks, I'll see if anybody else knows anything about it," as you walk away. You could mention that you overheard some students talking about it in the lunchroom or that you need to return a call to a parent regarding the situation. By dropping hints about parents or students, you are also deflecting attention away from her grade level peers. As you can imagine, she will become very concerned. By asking her to share, you are not disclosing what you know or do not know.

Additionally you can always revisit the situation. The next day you can start again by asking, "Mrs. Grump, can you tell me a little bit about a video last week and some cookies that some kids received?" You can reveal as much or as little as you would like. Eventually some semblance of the truth will come out. When it does, again act as if you are completely shocked that this could have happened. You might ask her to think overnight if she could call all 75 parents tomorrow and explain what happened. Your tone must be sincere and sound genuinely concerned. There can be no hint of rudeness or sarcasm. By asking her this at the end of the day she will have all evening to reflect.

Your conclusion will most likely be that she does not need to call the parents at this time, but under no circumstances should anything like this ever happen again in the school. Be aware that the longer you draw out the "investigation" and the questioning, the more it will make her uncomfortable and the more likely it will have an impact on her future behavior.

In any situation we face, we can initiate discussion with a teacher by asking, "Can you tell me a little bit about . . . ?" Understand that this is not an offensive approach. It could be used with your best teacher by asking, "Can you tell me a little bit about that science experiment you were doing? The students in the lunchroom were so excited about it."

It is essential that you be sensitive to the situations described previously. We are describing an intentional situation with a very mean-spirited staff member. Though the teacher may even make you a little nervous, this approach can allow you to have much more control of the direction of the conversation. It is also a technique you can refine by practicing it with students, parents, and other staff members. It allows them to do the talking, and this always helps people feel empowered when they do good things. However, it can raise discomfort for someone who has not done good things and is hoping to hide the truth.

## What Would the Best Teachers Do?

In Chapter 8, we describe dynamics that can occur at a faculty meeting, if we let them happen randomly. Difficult people can easily become empowered by sitting together, in the back, and near the door. This can be addressed by rearranging the room. Additionally, I used to have my assistant principal sit next to the most difficult teacher in the room. It is incredible how this makes that staff member uncomfortable and feel much less empowered as a result. Where did the idea come from? My best teachers.

If your school has all school student assemblies, what do different staff members do when they take their students to the gymnasium or auditorium? The best teachers sit right next to or in between the students who are most likely to be disruptive. These best teachers treat these challenging students as if they were the best students. They are polite and professional and, if appropriate, engage them in conversation about the assembly. They treat the students with respect and dignity and, in return, the students act respectful and dignified. This is the same thing an administrator accomplishes by sitting next to a disruptive teacher at a staff meeting. The administrator treats the staff member with respect and the staff member demonstrates respect.

The opposite also occurs at assemblies. The less effective classroom managers sit by other teachers, stand against the wall, or may not even attend the assembly. If they do sit with students, often the most disruptive students are farthest away. This same dynamic can occur with a less comfortable principal. The faculty in general could be far away, and the less cooperative teachers might have the most distance from an administrator.

We should ask ourselves what our best teachers do with students when they behave in a manner similar to our inappropriate teachers. By doing this, we can develop additional strategies with the adults in our school. Realize that the best teachers treat the students more like adults than anyone else in the school. They always treat them in a professional manner no matter how the students behave. As a result, the students behave more like adults in their classrooms than in any other setting in the school. By being aware of the behaviors and strategies our most talented teachers use, we can generate additional ideas that have proven effective in the classrooms. These can give us guidance when working with adults.

# Part 5

# Weakening the Influence of Difficult Teachers

# 14

# No More Party Poopers!

Nothing is more damaging to a school, especially one attempting to bring about positive change, than a negative teacher-leader. Someone with the capability of not only fighting good ideas, but worse, convincing other teachers to be negative is tremendously harmful. Sometimes these teachers are not particularly poor classroom teachers. They often have some interpersonal skills. These interpersonal strengths often increase their level of influence. However, you have to reduce their negative influence or it becomes very difficult to implement new programs or ideas. Many times if you can reduce their negative influence, you can tolerate them in the classroom.

The challenge of reducing their influence without losing credibility with the remainder of the faculty is difficult. It is also important not to diminish the relationship between the principal and this negative teacher leader. This negative leader may be able to damage the relationship between the principal and some of the staff members who look to this negative leader for guidance. For a school to more forward in an effective direction, it is essential to have the productive, positive staff members provide the momentum and direction for the school and staff. Reducing the ability of negative and resistant staff who cause other staff members to "drag their feet," is a critical part of this process.

The negative leaders in a school might be the most harmful influence in preventing school improvement. The teachers who are poor in the classroom or are ineffective in working with parents cause much consternation for the principal and have a negative impact on the school. Although intolerable, the influence of individual ineffective teachers is limited to the students they work with or the parents and community members they contact. Changing behavior is very important. If a principal truly wants to have schoolwide growth, the most detrimental, injurious staff members to the cause are the negative leaders in the school.

This section primarily focuses on the *informal* teacher-leader. The informal leaders are those staff members who have great impact when they speak at staff meetings or make "announcement" in the teachers' lounge. If a difficult teacher voices an opinion that, "We should not be going to block scheduling. I had a cousin whose school did and they now have terrible discipline in the school," others nod in agreement and actually follow the negative lead.

One teacher who resists change can be harmful. A negative leader who resists change and recruits others to fight change can be catastrophic to school improvement. The ability to reduce the influence that negative leaders have on other staff members is vital for the principal. If their detrimental impact can be limited, the school can progress apace.

Identifying the negative leaders may not be simple. Some negative leaders are publicly vocal and will be the first ones to speak out at faculty meetings or come to the principal's office to express their concerns about a new project or concept. Other negative influences are publicly neutral or may even seem positive. When the opportunity arises, however, the seemingly positive destructive leader will quickly make every effort to be a negative influence. There are many roles and styles of negative leaders.

**The Brown-Nosing Back Stabber.**   When a principal first takes a position, often a couple of teachers express their willingness to help in any way possible. These people will initially seem to be brown nosers. They are often trying to maintain or increase the power and influence they have among other teachers. These people are also attempting to be "in the know" so that they can have knowledge to influence their peers.

These negative leaders will seldom resist or express belligerence directly to the school leader. Instead they will often appear to be the opposite. Being aware of them is the first step in reducing the negative impact they have.

**The Town Crier.**   The town crier publicly argues against any possible positive change. Town criers are resistant and want everyone to know it. It is often a way for them to get attention. They are the "schoolhouse lawyers" at faculty meetings and committees. They are easy to identify. They often feel deprived, and expressing public criticism is a way for them to feel valuable. A more difficult task is to determine how many people agree with them. This is important, because sometimes town criers really have little or no support. They are often more loud than loved. They can drain enormous amounts of energy. Principals often feel the need to refute any of the issues or arguments they raise. Town criers often bring up age-old concerns. They will talk about issues that happened years ago—even issues that evolved under another leader. Perhaps, it reminds them of a time they took a leadership role that they felt other staff members valued. Perhaps they and colleagues felt the issue was dealt with unfairly. Town criers are most comfortable thinking that they carry the baton as champions of fairness.

**The Stay-At-Homes and Saboteurs.**   Phillip Schlechty (1993) recognizes five roles people play in school reform: trailblazers, pioneers, settlers, stay-at-homes, and saboteurs. The stay-at-homes resist change. They have insufficient confidence to alter what they are currently doing. These are the teachers that you believe have laminated lesson plans.

The stay-at-homes are not negative leaders. In fact, they have very little leadership ability at all. They are not often mean-spirited individuals. They usually lack the self-confidence to take risks of any kinds. The stay-at-homes often associate themselves with the more brazen saboteur. Saboteurs may have been more effective teachers. They might have been positive leaders. However, at some point they chose to fight school improvement by almost any means. They regularly play the devil's advocate. They are often the most vocal and belligerent negative staff members. Principals stay "logical" with saboteurs and hope to alter their views by providing information and facts. This approach is seldom effective with these negative leaders. However, if you can convert saboteurs, then their interpersonal abilities can be very beneficial. Realize that embittered people at work are embittered people at home. Although they may have "logical" reasons why everything the principal attempts to improve does not need improvement, these individuals fight every change.

There are many other types of detrimental leaders who can work in a school. The role of the principal in reducing their impact overlaps greatly no matter what the style of the negative leader.

Many times negative leaders are also less than sterling in the classroom. Although you want their classroom performance to improve, it is equally important to reduce their informal influence in the school. Affecting negative leaders' ability to lead is an essential element in reducing their influence. Realize that if you can reduce the support they have as informal leaders their discomfort level will increase and you will perhaps impact their classroom performance positively.

No matter what changes you hope occur in the negative leader's classroom performance, you need to reduce the detrimental impact very quickly. If you do not, then improving the school and its programs will be very difficult. It is important that the principal not allow a few—or even—one negative leader to prevent school growth.

## Understand the Dynamics—Dealing with Negative Leaders

Several some important concepts are essential to understanding the negative leader. The concepts pertain to the dynamics that surround a negative leader and colleagues. These dynamics involve the negative leader's impact on the followers and on the principal. Understanding these dynamics is essential to reducing the negative leader's impact.

In working with negative leaders, your instinctual reaction may not be the best. One of the quickest ways a principal can lose credibility is by arguing or getting into power struggles with faculty members. This is especially true if the argument or power struggle involves a school leader. Arguing on their level may dramatically increase their power. It is essential that principals do not lose their teachers' respect. Often, negative leaders will value attention of any kind. Getting into a power struggle, especially publicly, with challenging staff members, reinforces them. I am not sure whether this increases the negative leader's power, but I am confident that it diminishes the principal's effectiveness. Always remain professional and calm in these situations. The negative leader feels support at the time he or she chooses to make public comments. There will always be another opportunity to reduce this leader's negative influence more effectively. Remember, the principal does not have to prove who is in charge; everybody knows it. A principal has never *won* an argument, so do not get in them with these challenging staff— especially publicly.

Be aware that many negative leaders will instinctually disagree with any new concept. Teachers who publicly oppose change—especially those who have done so vehemently—may feel so embarrassed that if they change their minds they cannot publicly admit mistakes. Being aware of this can allow the principal to provide a way for them to save face. Without a way to save face, they may feel they have too much at stake to alter their stated viewpoint. If you avoid "drawing a line in the sand," then it is much more difficult for the negative leaders to end up in this position.

It is important to understand that it is impossible to lead without any followers. Your first thought may be to "take on" negative leaders. It is often clear who the informal group leaders are, and your reaction may be to try to "go after" the person who is preventing the school from progressing. However, before doing so, realize that in a negative group, leaders are usually the strongest persons. This may be because they are the most stubborn or because they feel that they have the least to lose. Whatever the situation, it is important to keep in mind that if they have no followers they cannot be negative leaders. Followers, negative or positive, are often less confident and more easily influenced than leaders. This is especially among negative teacher-leaders and followers. Many times the desire to follow is unrelated to the "cause" the negative leader carries. The follower may want to fit in. The follower may lack the confidence to disagree with a strong personality. The follower may have developed a friendship with the negative leader and feel allegiance to that friend. Being aware of these emotional ties may help a principal understand why using "reason" will not prevent the follower from emulating the negative leader.

Weak teachers who have regular contact with strong, negative colleagues may simply follow the negative leaders. These subordinate relations may have evolved because rooms are near each other, or conference periods coincide. The followers and leaders might teach at the same grade level or in the same department.

Schlechty (1993) described stay-at-homes and saboteurs. The stay-at-homes are generally afraid of change. When they feel discomfort due to an impending change, they may align themselves with the most vocal resistants, the saboteurs, even if they do not agree with reasons for resistance or respect the saboteurs at all.

Being aware of the weaker constitutions may help in reducing the negative leaders' influence. Teachers who follow negative leaders often just want to follow someone. Developing as many opportunities and scenarios for the negative followers to become connected to more positive staff members can dramatically limit the impact and influence of negative leaders.

# Break Up the Group

The safest and most effective way to reduce the influence of negative leaders is to reduce the number of their followers. Rather than attempting to go "head on" with negative leaders and risking martyrdom, diminish their influence by decreasing the number of supporters. There is emotional "strength in numbers"; reducing these numbers may provide opportunities to work directly and productively with the negative leaders.

We often assume that people who spend a lot of time together respect and like each other. In most cases this is true. However, among a group of difficult teachers mutual respect and friendship might be absent. Although they may associate with each other regularly, keep in mind that these people generally do not have a great number of lovable characteristics. The morning club of complainers will just as quickly talk badly about the teacher in their group who is absent that day as they would the principal. They are often not friends; they are more like a "loser support group."

Compare working with this tight-knit group of teachers with managing three students who are close friends and who were referred to the office together for inappropriate behavior. If you let all three of them sit together while waiting to see you and if you deal with the trio simultaneously, they will feel much more power and confidence in standing up to you. If, on the other hand, you make them wait for you in separate offices and deal with them individually they are usually much more compliant and much less brash. The same is true in working with a group of difficult teachers. Make every attempt to work with one at a time. You want them to feel as lonely as possible.

There is an old saying that, "water finds its own level." The most effective people seek out other high achievers to associate and collaborate with. The same is true of the more negative people. Difficult teachers often associate most closely with other difficult individuals. They have lower regard for students, their profession, and themselves. They can find comfort with their peers.

At many schools, the most negative people sit at the same

table for coffee or lunch. As discussed earlier, they gravitate toward each other at staff meetings. If you can reduce the mem-
bership of these "gripe clubs," you can substantially reduce their
impact. It is almost impossible for anyone to be cynical alone.

Here is a hypothetical example. At a school, a group of less
positive staff members gathered each morning for coffee. There
were one or two negative leaders in this group and several followers who had weaker personalities. One day the principal
asked a weaker follower, who taught social studies, to attend a
meeting at another school. When they arrived at the other school,
a social studies teacher was holding class in the parking lot. The
students were gathered in a taped outline of Christopher
Columbus's boat, the Nina. This taped outline was the same size
as the actual boat, which was very small.

As you can imagine, this is a wonderful concept. Regardless
of whether the students could memorize the number of crew-
men and the exact number of days sailing, they will never
forget that it was a pretty small boat that held quite a few people
for a very long time. This was the point of the lesson. Suppose
your social studies teacher was just getting ready to start a unit
on the "Discovery of America" and you suggested that she do
this same thing. Despite her resistance, you even volunteered to
come in over the weekend and tape the boat yourself. Assuming that teacher was a follower with a less domineering personality and you were visiting one on one with her, there is a good
chance she would acquiesce—especially if you would do all the
work.

Imagine her surprise, on Monday morning, when she reluc-
tantly takes her first class to the parking lot to sail in the *Nina*
and finds the local television station ready to tape the activity.
The local newspaper photographer is there also. In addition, the
student newspaper and the principal were taking pictures. Both
the local and student paper put the pictures on the front page
and there was a story on the local news. It was the first feature
in the *Friday Focus*. The teacher felt more pride than she had
ever felt in her entire career. Ironically, the morning coffee group
did not want her sitting with them any more. Once she had done

something positive for kids, she was no longer welcome among them. That may sound sad, but as you can imagine, the more positive staff members welcomed her with open arms. That teacher now had so much pride that she had no desire to join the coffee club again. One small step for a teacher, one giant leap for . . . children and the school.

I learned a similar lesson regarding the importance of keeping a negative from growing. I had a teacher who was very negative. His conference period was first thing in the morning. He consistently arrived quite late. Thinking I was very clever, I scheduled his planning period later in the day for the next year. There was no animosity over this, it was a very public decision after reexamining the scheduling.

The next year he had students starting at 8:00. Unfortunately, he would arrive by 7:30. I say unfortunately, because he took a prime position at the negative table. So while I had reduced the gripe group by several my first year, I also added to it by providing the group with a new recruit. By altering the schedule of this difficult teacher I not only added a member to this group, but he assumed a leadership role. Having learned my lesson, I rescheduled him to have his early planning period the next year.

I could have waited in the parking lot and documented his tardiness, but I do not believe in this type of leadership style. So, for the time being, I chose to live with his lateness to benefit the school.

The end of the day posed similar problems. On Friday afternoons, many staff members are anxious to leave as soon as possible. Some of the negative staff make every attempt to be the first ones out the door. Your instinctive reaction may be to stop them, but I say, "Let them go." Again, are you better off, for it is worse to have them in school. You might even be tempted to start their cars for them. Obviously I am kidding, but be aware of the importance of picking and choosing where you decide to put your energies.

If the behaviors of the negative teachers are impacting positive staff members, then this situation would need to be addressed. Realize that rules and policies often have little effect on difficult teachers. They are the *least* likely to abide by them. If there is a policy or rule in place, effective staff members may come upset that some are "getting away with it." Sometimes the solution is not to try to "catch" the difficult teacher, but to change the policy, especially if it has no value.

Our teachers were required to stay 30 minutes after the school day was over. However, some of the less effective faculty would leave earlier, especially on Friday. This truly does not bother me, because I am much more concerned about effectiveness and performance than I am about following rules. If this negatively affected positive faculty, then I would have dealt with this issue. Knowing it did affect my best staff members I addressed it. In each *Friday Focus* my last line was, "Feel free to leave at 3:05 today. Have a great weekend!" It is amazing what perception does. No one in the school left any earlier. But there were two differences. The teachers who always departed early no longer had to sneak. More importantly, my positive faculty were no longer upset, because others were not breaking a rule! In addition, they enjoyed the flexibility of leaving earlier to start the weekend, even though they seldom did. Sometimes breaking up a negative group is easier than you might think. Any day that negative staff vacate the building early is probably a positive day for the school.

In addition to reducing the size of the group, be aware of the emotional impact that a group can have. I will go into more detail on this in Part 7, but realize the importance of a difficult teacher "feeling" alone when you are attempting to alter behavior or dismiss them. Again, I am talking about the most dominant, resistant people—the real hard-core negative staff members. This feeling is the reason you want to work with negative teachers one at a time. The more alone they feel, the more uncomfortable they will feel. This makes them much less likely to resist change. In addition to not limiting the size of the group, don't allow ineffective teachers to develop an emotional bond among themselves by dealing with more than one of them at a time. This is especially true, if you are initiating a more formal dismissal documentation process.

## The Power of Pity

If you are truly attempting to reduce the impact of a negative leader, the simplest way is to help bring to light the true feelings the staff should have for this person. This process is not easy. If you have a negative leader in your school and you wonder why anyone would want to follow this person's lead, you probably have a difficult leader whose influence may be dramatically reduced by the power of pity.

If a person is cynical, bitter, and negative, reactions to this person are anger, hurt, or aggression. However, as caring people, the feeling we should have is empathy. You should feel pity for this person. You do not want to be around the difficult teachers for even five minutes. Almost every contact with them is unpleasant. Not only is this true for you, it is true for everyone around them. If you do not want to be around these people for five minutes a day, just think how they must feel. They have to be around themselves 24 hours a day! No wonder they are cynical, negative, and bitter.

It is essential to provide the remainder of your staff the opportunity to realize that pity is what they should feel for these unhappy individuals. Helping everyone in your school to come to this realization is a valuable method for reducing the influence of your most negative leader. If we can help develop a sympathetic perspective among the whole staff, this can dramatically affect this difficult person's leadership. No one wants to follow someone they pity.

I want to share a story regarding the most powerful negative leader I had ever worked with. I will refer to him as Mr. Crawford. This teacher was both an overt and a covert negative leader. When I discussed new programs with faculty members, he loved to chime in, "It won't work! It did not work back in '49, it will not work now!" The discouraging part for me was not his statement; rather it was the reaction of other staff members. It was amazing how he could bellow, "it won't work," and see this sentiment quickly reverberate throughout many of the other staff—including some of the positive teachers. I was always taken

aback when this would occur. I was also never quite able to figure out where this influence came from.

Crawford's covert influence was less obvious, but it was at
least as powerful. I became aware of this through a variety of
occurrences. One day a couple of staff members and I were sitting around very informally after school. We were not even discussing school matters (a miracle!), and one of the teachers
brought up a question about the possibility of remodeling an
old storage area into a computer lab writing center. This storage
area was stacked to the brim with stuff that had not been moved
in decades. I mentioned that I would be happy to ask our
maintenance director about the possibility of having the area
remodeled. Two of the teachers excitedly said that they had just
read about a grant program that would support the funding of
technology for innovative programs. They even added that they
would be happy to write the grant for the school. The handful
of very positive people we had in the room started brainstorm-
ing all sorts of different ideas and benefits of the concept. There
was quite a bit of energy established in a short period of time. I
told them I would check into the remodeling the next day.

The next morning during her planning time, one of my most
innovative, energetic, and positive teachers came to my office
with slumped shoulders and said with great despair, "Forget
about checking with the maintenance director. We will not be
allowed to do the remodeling."

I asked why and she said, "We were discussing the idea this
morning and someone said the maintenance director had been
asked about it before and was not interested." I requested a little
more information about who had asked and when. She shared
that Mr. Crawford said someone had inquired before and they
were told, "no."

That day I asked Mr. Crawford, "Someone mentioned that
you had some information about the old storage room. Can you
tell me a little bit about the attempts to remodel it previously?"

Mr. Crawford stammered around and eventually I was able
to drag out of him that more than 20 years ago he thought that
someone had asked someone somewhere about the possibility

of using that storage area for some purpose. He thought the request had been declined.

My discouragement was not in his approach; I expected that. I was frustrated by his great influence among so many others in the school. This was especially difficult to accept when his influence reached positive leaders. I knew that I had to diminish his impact on other teachers in order for us to sustain any positive energies.

I would like to share a little more information about Mr. Crawford. If you ever asked him how he was doing, he would answer in his overbearing and harsh manner, "Terrible, I am doing terrible." Two of his favorite discussion topics were baseball and the weather, both of which were always lousy. He had two baseball teams to complain about, even though both of them were in first place.

Here is an example of his influence using one of his favorite topics: the weather. One day before school started in August, Mr. Crawford was visiting with two of our winter sport coaches. Mr. Crawford told them, "You better watch out in basketball season this year. I read in the *Farmer's Almanac* that we are going to have a lot of snow in January."

In later conversations with me the coaches explained that, "We need to be prepared to reschedule a lot of games this basketball season. We heard it was going to be a terrible winter this year." These stories help represent the impact this one person had on the culture of the school. He dramatically reduced the opportunity for positive staff members to be productive. After much deliberation, I thought of an approach I wanted to try. I had to attempt to put the positive people in charge of the school.

At a faculty meeting, I told the staff about my new next-door neighbor. The new neighbor was an older gentlemen who was incredibly similar to Mr. Crawford. I shared this story about my neighbor:

> We had a new next-door neighbor move in and I was thinking about him the other day. It is important for me, like it is for most people, to be friendly and wel-

coming to people who are new to town. So the first day I saw my new neighbor I smiled, waved, and said, "How are you doing?" He responded with a frown on his face, "Terrible, I am doing terrible." I thought something was truly wrong so I went over and asked if I could assist with anything, and he coldly said "no."

I thought to myself. This guy must really hate me. But I was not about to give up. I decided I would bring up one of my favorite subjects, baseball. So when I saw him the next day, I smilingly said, "How about those St. Louis Cardinals! They are in first place." His typical gruff reply was, "The Cardinals are the worst team in baseball!"

His tone and manner were very unfriendly, but being stubborn in nature I thought to myself, "He must be an American League fan." Hoping still to build a friendly relationship, I switched teams and said to my neighbor, "The Kansas City Royals won again last night."

Once again in his typical unfriendly manner he shot back, "Remember what I said about the Cardinals? I was wrong, the Royals are even worse."

Knowing better than to revisit the sports scene again, the next time I saw my neighbor outside was on a gorgeous day. Heading out to my car, I cheerfully shared, "Pretty day isn't it!" Mr. Friendly responded curtly, "No, we need rain."

Thinking I would give it one more shot, a few days later it was raining when I was getting ready to head off to work. Jogging to the car, I saw my neighbor looking out his front door. I smiled and said, "Hey, we got that rain you wanted!' He coarsely growled, "Wrong kind of rain!"

I then shared with my faculty, "You know at first, I thought my neighbor just hated me. Then after mentioning the Cardinals and the Royals, I thought maybe he just dislikes baseball. Finally after our last two weather conversations, I figured he just had it in for Mother Nature. I then realized that there was just one person he disliked. And who was that?"

The faculty responded as a whole, "Himself. He disliked himself."

And I shared my final thought in the gentlest and most empathic tone, "Every time I was around this person, I felt worse. For a while, based upon the way he was treating me, I thought I must have done something to offend him. Then I finally came to the conclusion that I was not going to let myself be affected by him anymore. He is not going to make any of my days a bad day. He is not going to waste any of my life's time."

I closed by sharing, "I realized that instead of being mad at my neighbor, the real feeling I should have for him is pity. But even though he has chosen to waste his life being angry, bitter, and miserable, I am not going to let him waste any more of mine."

Of course, in addition to describing my neighbor I was describing Mr. Crawford. Everyone in the room saw Mr. Crawford in my neighbor and realized what they had been letting him do to them for years. I thought when the faculty left the meeting that day they were going to go and pat Mr. Crawford on the head on their way out. In addition to realizing that they were not going to let him affect their lives anymore in a negative way, they realized what an unhappy life he had chosen to lead. Never again did he have the ability to be a major negative influence in the school. People will not follow someone they pity. Pity is truly the emotion we should feel for the unhappy people we know in our lives and in our schools.

This approach may not initially alter the behavior of the teacher you are describing. However, more importantly, it takes away this person's ability to influence other staff members.

## Guest Speakers

Stories like the story about my "neighbor" are sometimes very difficult to share with your own staff members. However, they are usually very easy to convey to strangers or people we know less well. This is the reason that guest speakers can be so powerful in reducing the influence of the most difficult staff members.

If you are fortunate enough to be in a wealthy school district, you may have the budget to support these efforts. You may even be able to bring in nationally regarded experts. However, for many of us, funding for speakers is often minimal or absent. One effective strategy is staff development that principals can provide each other. Rather than hiring an unknown commodity to make a point, bringing in peers from another school or district can be powerful. They can use examples tailored to your school. In payment, you can work with staff at the visiting principals' school.

The speaker can use specific examples necessary for your teachers. If an "outsider" shared the neighbor story or another story that could highlight the feelings we should have for difficult teachers, you might accomplish enlightenment without putting yourself on the spot.

Having an outsider help provide perspective for your faculty is very valuable. If a speaker can help your staff see the ineffectiveness of a negative leader, you can reduce the negative influence. If your negative leader abuses the copier, the speaker could share a personal example about a poor teacher who would call in sick whenever the photocopier was broken. Helping everyone to see the devastating abilities negative staff members hold can diminish the influence they hold over their followers.

I will share an example from a school where I was recently a guest speaker. When I first started the workshop, I noticed a person whose body language was very negative. Any time the other faculty spoke, this person would roll her eyes or sigh. Several of the staff who saw her do this were obviously uncomfortable. They had no desire to speak up and risk incurring her indirect wrath. In addition, I noticed that she was grading papers and pretending to be disinterested in workshop activities. Appearing disinterested was obviously an emotional shield for her, because she was keenly aware of all that was taking place. When she disagreed with something, she was quick to reflect her contempt in a reaction. It was clear that the positive people were the most uncomfortable and this person was exerting a great deal of negative, informal influence over the group.

When we took our first break, I asked the principal about this teacher. The principal shared information that you would expect about someone who behaved in this fashion: This teacher was the scorn of the entire school. The principal was intimidated by this person. This teacher was also very belligerent toward students. The remainder of the faculty was oppressed by her domineering nature. As a guest speaker, I had an opportunity to reverse the discomfort levels. I wanted her to become less comfortable and to reduce the negative influence she had on the faculty.

We were doing a team building activity and I asked the group, "What would you do, if you were on a team with a member whom no one liked? The students did not want to be assigned to this teacher. None of the other faculty wanted to work with this teacher. What if this teacher's body language and demeanor were offensive? During meetings this person grades papers and acts indifferently, yet sighs and makes snide remarks when others make good positive suggestions." As I talked, I walked around the room and ended up directly behind this teacher.

Please be aware that I was very positive when we were talking. Yet, I was very aware of her body language, her grading papers, and her sighing and comments. As an outsider, I could approach things in this neutral manner. Interestingly, she put her grade book away and at least pretended to be interested the rest of the meeting. In future contacts with the principal, he indicated that she has never brought her grade book to a staff meeting again.

This intimidating behavior by a negative staff member cannot be allowed to subdue the positive faculty. A principal may not feel comfortable addressing these issues with staff; an outsider may be more comfortable and influential in doing so.

# 15

# Sometimes You Have To Shuffle the Deck

## Room Location

Sometimes external factors determine which staff members spend the most time together. One factor that often affects the development of informal relationships is room location. If a follower has a room located next to or near a negative leader, this can easily encourage support for the negative teacher. Working with the dynamics of factors such as room location can help cultivate an appropriate school culture. Altering room locations can affect this dynamic in a positive way.

Three teachers at one of my schools had classrooms at the end of one hallway. These teachers could hardly wait to see each other at the end of each class period in order to complain about their last classes, their next classes, or something else. Their tone in the morning was negative. I internally referred to this part of the school as "crabs' corner."

I realized that this room configuration had been in place for years. The tone they established with each other carried over into their contact with the students. These three were also quite inappropriately confrontational with students in the hallways. I studied the dynamic among these teachers and finally determined that the only way to change this behavior was to change their room locations. I knew that one of these three was the negative leader. However, I was also aware that if I moved the leader only, the other two would continue to be negative simply out of habit.

I had the good fortune of beginning our first interdisciplinary team the next year. This cozy room location was the ideal spot to move the team. So, after much deliberation we moved several teachers' classrooms and split up these three individuals. One of them continued to attempt to gripe. However, this leader was now so isolated that she was unable to influence anyone. The other two were now with new peers who did not address concerns ineffectively in the hallway. So they taught happily ever after.

Be aware that your positive people are your most important staff members when "shuffling the deck." Do not make their workdays miserable by surrounding them with several negative staff members. I would not move a backbone or superstar teacher without approval. It is essential that you do not harm them at the expense of working with the most challenging faculty members.

## Conference Period—Planning Time

Planning period and lunch break proximity can be as destructive as classroom locations. Being sensitive to this can help establish how negative leaders and followers develop their relationships. Taking advantage of the opportunity to affect this dynamic when the chance arises can dramatically affect the culture and climate of a conference or lunch period. This small effect may carry over into the environment of the entire school.

At the high-school level, there might be annual opportunities to develop new schedules. However, some powerful teachers might insist on having a fifth period conference each year. These are often established for the teacher's benefit rather than for the benefit of the students or school. Here is one approach that may allow you to reschedule conference periods, if they have long been established.

At a staff meeting, ask how many of the faculty have unbalanced classes. In other words, ask whether any have one class of 14 and then 32 the next hour. Feel free to use whatever numbers that occur at your school. Then ask the group how many feel that more balanced classes might be beneficial. Several hands will likely go up. Next, share that you would like to rebuild the schedule from scratch and that one possible change is the alteration of conference times. Ask the staff to let you know of any barriers that might prevent scheduling alterations that could result in more balanced classes for everyone in the school. If this conference time is critical to any of your positive staff either do not change theirs or visit with them privately about change that would benefit their schedule. If you routinely change the schedule each year, then simply be aware of whose conference periods fall when.

Another issue regarding rescheduling planning entails asking these questions. Is it better to divide the negative teachers so that each group must deal with one of them? Or is it better to schedule several less effective people together so that no one else has to share the staff workroom? Weighing the potential effects of these options can help you make a more informed decision. Being aware of these times at an elementary school is also important. There may not be regular chances to alter the common time teachers share because planning periods might be determined by grade level.

## Grade Level

The grade-level dynamic at an elementary school is critical. If teachers in one grade are less progressive or ineffective, they may hold the entire school from moving forward. More importantly, they reduce the learning opportunities for the students in that grade. An important issue in considering grade level movement among teachers is to make sure that the positive and progressive staff understand that you value their assistance in moving grades. If you consider plans to place a negative among positive staffers, be sure that the effective teachers support your strategy before finalizing decisions and making them public. The positive staff members and their morale are too important to sacrifice casually.

Similar considerations regarding breaking up the group could also involve the lunch periods during which staff members eat and the recess times during which teachers work together. Obviously a principal cannot and probably does not want to try to control all of these schedule items with difficult teachers being the only consideration. Keeping in mind the dynamics schedules can create may be an important factor in redirecting the influence of some difficult staff members.

## If You Miss a Little, You Miss a Lot

As previously mentioned, withholding power from negative people is paramount. In the example of the voluntary summer workshop, a large percentage of teachers were about to hand over power to teachers who were not even attending the workshop. A principal can take advantage of these opportunities when negative people pick and choose which meetings and activities they attend. During their absence you can reduce their influence.

Optional meetings open to all staff offer exceptional opportunities to reduce negative influences. The nice part about an approach like this is that people who are interested can come; others stay away. If negative people choose not to participate, not only will the meetings go better but you can reduce their power of resistance at later meetings. At a subsequent meeting when you are discussing a decision made at an optional meeting be aware of the difficult people who were absent. When they attempt to express their opposition to a new idea feel free to add, "Well we decided that at the planning meeting last week. Oh, you chose not to attend." Do not speak sarcastically. Speak emphatically with neutrality, which will subdue their power to argue with the decision. Again, keep in mind that you want to treat people as though they want to do what is right. Share that you hope to see them at the next planning meeting. You cannot allow negative people to detract from the work that many of their peers did voluntarily.

Having open-ended voluntary discussions and planning sessions can dramatically reduce the influence of negative staff. Having principal advisory committees or leadership teams in which every staff member can participate is a valuable way to empower the positive staff members who are most likely to attend. Since anyone *can* participate, they give up their power by choosing not to. This voluntary structure is a productive and open way to place the balance of power with the hardest working and most dedicated faculty in the school.

# Part 6

# The Role of New Faculty

# 16

# What About the New Kids?

New teachers can be powerful tools in improving schools. New staff members can play essential roles in the growth of a school. It is critical that the principal provide guidance and structure to insure that the new faculty members have the greatest positive impact possible on the school and that they are *never* influenced by negative teachers.

There are really only two ways to improve your school. One is to improve the teachers that you have. The other is to hire better ones. When you have the chance to hire a new staff member, you maximize the opportunity. It is much easier to hire a good teacher than it is to fire a bad one.

When principals hire a new teacher, they should be more interested in the school becoming like the new teacher than in the new teacher becoming like the school. If no programs assure this, then the development of the new faculty member will be left to chance. These new staff members are too essential to *hope* that they become positive, contributing faculty members. (Remember that no college has a course on griping in the teachers' lounge, yet somehow, a few new teachers have that ability refined by Thanksgiving.) A further challenge with new staff goes far beyond preventing them from becoming negative: Cultivate them to become positive leaders and superstars in the shortest time possible. There is no guarantee that a new staff member will quickly assume a leadership role, but there are many things that a principal can do to greatly enhance these opportunities.

First, make sure new staff members become members of the positive faculty. Examine some of the informal social structures in the school, then determine how new staff can fit into positive groups. Determining classroom proximity can initiate some of the relationships they will build. By the same token, conference period peers and grade-level or departmental assignments can have impact on whom they influence or by whom they are influenced. You should also keep in mind faculty meeting dynamics and where new members will sit during meetings.

If a new faculty member does not feel that he or she fits in at school, which group will always add another member? The negative teachers always have room for one more. Rather than hope a new teacher declines to join a negative group at a staff meeting, link the recent hire with productive staff members. This is often doubly important if gender, department, grade level, or some other affinity is involved. A principal might ask a superstar, "Did you ever feel awkward or funny at your first faculty meeting as a new staff member? I was thinking back to my first year as a teacher and how awkward I felt. Do you think that Mary (the new teacher) might feel that way? Do you have any idea how we might help her?" The superstar will generally volunteer to ask the new teacher to sit nearby at the faculty meeting. This can help ensure that the new member fits in and begins to establish rapport with a positive influence.

Many schools have mentor programs for new faculty and staff. These programs pair up new staff members with experienced teachers. If this teacher can be linked with a superstar, this may be most beneficial. Sometimes there are grade-level and subject area restrictions placed on the partners that can be linked through these programs. Although these can be positive programs, they may provide just a part of the introduction that will benefit new staff members most.

The principal can establish a new-staff orientation program. Plan an informational program to be offered before the new year starts. Continue to reinforce the program goals during the school year. One year I had eight new staff members in my school. It was very important to me that new faculty support and even lead a new culture that we were developing in the school. Rather than just hope they would build relations with the positive staff members, we established a new-staff orientation program that continued through the first 12 weeks of school. Every other Tuesday morning an hour before school started, I met with the eight new faculty. These meetings allowed the new staff members to develop relationships among themselves and with me. They allowed them to become their own peer support group. They were able to reciprocate and encourage each other's energy and enthusiasm. The efforts to introduce them to the other positive faculty were supported during these meetings. The new faculty associated themselves more closely with many of the positive staff members. The existing staff members enhanced their relations with the new staff as well.

These sessions focused on a variety of areas. Holding orientation over 12 weeks made the introduction less overwhelming than a traditional one-day introduction. We offered orientations on classroom management. Two of my most effective staff members and role models led the sessions. The most dynamic counselor in the school directed the session covering counseling. The most effective special education teachers in the school explained special education programs. Each of the six sessions was designed to help orient the new staff to our school and programs. Perhaps more importantly, it continued to expand the growing base of positive and dynamic educators we had in the school.

A greater challenge is helping to develop the positive leadership abilities in new teachers, if they are entering a school that has a large number of negative staff. Improving school culture with new teachers is more complex and probably even more critical than simply ensuring they build relations with positive faculty members.

# 17

# New Teacher Leadership

I believe that the induction and orientation of new staff members does not start at the first meeting after they are hired. This process must begin during the interview. Hiring new teachers capable of being school leaders requires selecting people with leadership ability. Once selected, you must offer opportunities for them to develop confidence and support them as they assume leadership.

If I were employing a teacher whose classroom would be next to a negative leader, I would explore this in the first interview. I would ask the candidate, "What would you do if your classroom were next to a person who would put pressure on you to do the absolute minimum you could as a teacher?" Or I would ask this teacher about any potential situation that might present itself. I would want to know before I considered hiring, because I would need someone who could be self-confident. I would need a teacher who would do the right thing despite the expectations of a more experienced peer. This would provide me with an opportunity to establish my expectations for a new staff member faced with challenging situations.

A similar questioning strategy is effective for hiring and cultivating teacher-leaders. You want to hire individuals with leadership strengths and then provide opportunities and structures for these skills to be maximized. When contacting references about potential hires, ask about their leadership skills. Try to determine from these contacts whether this person is a leader or a follower. Ask the references what they think the applicant would do if the candidate's room were next to a negative teacher who pressured the prospect to do the minimum and leave work as early as possible. There is an excellent chance that the contact has worked with negative people and can offer valuable insight on how the candidate would deal with such a situation.

Explain to potential teachers during interviews what you need, and be clear. Explain that you need candidates to help lead the school to improve the climate, culture, or whatever program that is most significant to the growth of your school. During the interview, ask whether they can provide this. Ask leadership-situation questions. Determining this ability before hiring teachers can be much more effective than hiring with hope they have this ability.

It is also important that you empower new teachers to begin to assume informal leadership roles. I shared with all new teachers I was considering that, "We do not have a pecking order here. I want whomever I hire to share their opinions as soon as they feel comfortable. I need your fresh ideas and input. I am going to hire applicants because I want my school to become more like them." This was very powerful information that I would reemphasize in the first meeting after employing new teachers. I wanted this expectation to be a positive morale and confidence builder for all new staff members. They valued this conversation and shared with me many times that it assisted them in feeling integral to the school and staff very quickly.

An open teaching position may be the most precious commodity a principal can have. Employing a great teacher for the students is critical. Hiring a positive leader/superstar may be the most important factor in the school improvement process. If a school loses a negative staff member and gains a dynamic teacher, improvement in the school is immediate and dramatic. Not only is the school a better place to be for the students, but it is also more positive for everyone else in the building.

# Part 7

# Eliminating Difficult Teachers

# 18

# Where Do I Start?

It is a great day when a difficult teacher leaves a school. When even one negative staff member exits, the school dynamics can change completely. Faculty can finally have a new peer with whom they can be proud to work. The principal's burden has been greatly lightened. The support staff can once again be treated with the respect that they deserve, and often the respect for the principal from the central office can skyrocket. But most importantly, the students in that school can now have the quality teacher they deserve.

Although this section includes some information regarding formal dismissal of difficult teachers, it centers around many alternative methods of eliminating ineffective staff members. The alternatives may take less time and energy on the part of the principal than formal dismissal. If there is an alternative to documenting, remediation, documenting more, due process hearings, and other procedures that the teacher is allowed, then give them a try. However, if nothing else works then dismissal is inevitable. The principal must roll up his or her sleeves and do what is best for the students and the school. Before you get to that point, consider some of the issues that a principal faces in eliminating the most difficult faculty.

## Focus on the End Goal

An essential element in eliminating a difficult teacher is keeping sight of the real goal. Covey (1989) exhorts readers to, "[b]egin with the end in mind." Your goal is to eliminate a particular behavior. The teacher could choose to discontinue inappropriate behavior. In most situations you can achieve this discontinuation. However, if a teacher chooses ineffectiveness, then you must eliminate the teacher from your school. Keeping the goal in mind can help you accomplish a couple of objectives.

One benefit of focusing on a particular result is that it allows you to monitor the teacher's behavior. If a teacher chooses to alter his or her behavior in a positive way, then you have accomplished your goal. If you lose sight of your goal and the teacher alters behavior(s), you might still put limited time and valuable energy into a battle that you have already won.

Focus will prevent you from getting into power struggles. In other words, if you want to eliminate certain behaviors you don't have to eliminate the teacher—just the behavior. I have witnessed principals become so angry at a teacher that the only thing they wanted to do was fire the teachers. These principals have become so emotional that when poor teachers have threatened to quit, the principals convince them to stay just so they can dismiss them. These administrators lost sight of their goal. Instead their goal became revenge. As a starting point, the principal must establish what is needed in order to consider results successful. Remove personality from the equation; focus on behavior. Deciding which faculty member to start with may be an even tougher decision.

## Eenie, Meenie, Minie, Moe

A challenging determination is where to start—especially when a principal inherits a school with several difficult staff members. Earlier I discussed the reasoning behind working with some negative followers prior to taking on a negative leader. However, in light of this situation there are several factors to consider: whether the teacher cares about being liked, what level of peer support there is, and which difficult teacher will throw in the towel first. A seemingly obvious decision might be to start with your worst teacher. This may sound most reasonable, but there may be other factors to balance against this.

In the section regarding making the difficult teacher uncomfortable, I described the concept of using peers. I discussed asking your difficult teachers whether they cared what their peers thought about them. If so, it might be appropriate to put more pressure on them with that approach than to spend your energy attempting to get them out of the building. I believe that if you have staff members—no matter how difficult—who have even a minimal regard for what their peers think, then you may be able to find an approach that could be more immediate and require less of the principal's energy.

In determining which difficult teacher to eliminate first, identify which negative staff member has the least peer support. If you eliminate an unpopular teacher, there is less impetus for unrest among the staffers. Dismissing more highly regarded teachers—regardless of their ineffectiveness—will often generate more fallout for the principal. This can be true both during the process and afterward. Secondly, a person who feels unsupported is much less likely to resist the principal. The more lonely they feel during the time you work to eliminate them the less strength they have to fight the process.

Successfully finding the path of least resistance (that is, rapidly dismissing one difficult teacher) gets the attention of many others. This can cause other challenging staff members to change their behavior without even getting to the point of working to eliminate them. This is one of the ultimate ways of making difficult staff members feel uncomfortable. This applies to principals in schools with several teachers who should be dismissed. Putting your energies where they will have the most positive results should be a factor in your decision as to which teacher to start with. This is not carte blanche to dismiss an average teacher just to prove your mettle. It should only be used with teachers who need to be dismissed.

For example, a principal was hired to work in a school with a challenging staff. The previous leader was viewed as being quite ineffective. As is often the case, if there is a perceived lack of leadership many people try to fill the void. In a school with a principal who is perceived as an ineffective leader, teachers with dominant personalities often assume vast informal power. When a new principal is employed, the new administrator faces the daunting task of attempting to reduce the influence of this powerful negative leader. Ineffective leadership is, without question, the primary cause of the emergence of difficult teachers. This is true both in the hiring process and in creating environments in which ineffectiveness is tolerated—or unknowingly, even encouraged.

This new principal faced the prospect of building a positive school culture with many self-anointed negative leaders. This principal interviewed all teachers informally during the summer prior to the start of his first year. This is a beneficial activity. The meetings should be relaxed and yet have purpose (Whitaker and Lumpa). During these interviews the principal discovered that *all* of the teachers had great contempt for the secretary. She was hired the previous year and had insulted every teacher. The principal was glad to hear this, because the secretary had insulted him several times during their first month together. Of more concern to the principal was the way that the secretary addressed the parents and students who came to enroll at the school during the summer months. After conversing with all the teachers, the principal gave the secretary some improvement directives. The secretary ignored them and was dismissed. When the teachers came back to start school, there was a new secretary employed.

This empowered the most effective staff by making them feel that they were listened to. More importantly, many of the difficult teachers quickly decided to improve their efforts because of the principal's ability to take prompt and decisive action with the secretary. This caused many of the potentially difficult staff members to be on their best behavior. Because the secretary was universally disliked there was not the backlash that might be expected following a swift change under new leadership.

One challenge in eliminating a difficult teacher is reducing others' regard for their colleague. If effective teachers can observe an ineffective colleague—even for an hour—they will quickly realize the teacher lacks skill. Then their support for this person as a professional will likely diminish and there will be less resistance toward the principal's efforts.

Developing an exchange program or a "school tour" for all staff to visit each other's classes are two ways to increase the awareness of the lesser capabilities of a fellow teacher. Strong staff members will eagerly participate in such a program, thereby reducing their concern when you begin to focus on the behaviors of an individual teacher. It can also increase the discomfort that other difficult teachers feel, because of a heightened awareness of the similarities between themselves and the teacher who is under fire.

# 19

# Retirement and Other Miracles

## Retirement

When difficult teachers retire, it is like finding a pot of gold at the end of a rainbow. You always hope it is there, yet you have to be careful not to get your hopes too high. Being aware of when your difficult people are eligible to retire is important. But also realize that as much as they seem to dislike their job they carry this unhappiness with them all of the time; they may not retire when eligible. A difficult teacher's spouse may not be looking forward to having this person around all of the time either. Difficult people are often miserable. Generally they do not particularly enjoy being around themselves. They keep working at school because no one else would hire them and perhaps they don't look forward to pursuing other interests.

The principal can assist teachers into making a decision to retire earlier than they might choose independently. If a difficult teacher is eligible for retirement, the best possibility of eliminating this teacher is retirement. With difficult teachers it *seems* as though they retired years ago, they just have not notified anyone of it yet.

Marv Levy, former coach of the Buffalo Bills, was frequently asked when he would retire. One day he responded, "Those people who always talk about when they are going to retire probably already have." I used this quote in my *Friday Focus* because I had a teacher who would use the threat of retirement as a weapon. When he did not want to do something that would require extra work he would readily offer, "It does not matter to me; I will be retired by then anyhow." Yet if something else were being considered for five years in the future and he wanted to sabotage it, he would just as quickly offer, "It won't work—it didn't work back in '46." After I put that quote in the *Friday Focus*, he never publicly talked about retirement again. After years of threatening, he finally decided to quit. It seemed like a fitting resolution.

I was once principal at a school that included an offensive librarian, Mrs. Dewey. Her theory of librarianship was, "Don't touch the books; they are all in order." It was not the most conducive approach to utilizing the media center. I knew that she had more than enough years of service to be eligible to retire. In addition, her husband had just retired. On top of that, the school district had a one-year-only retirement incentive for which she qualified. I was thinking for sure that this would be her final year.

Rather than leaving it to chance, I knew that I had to find out whether she was going to retire. I was afraid that if I asked Mrs. Dewey whether she were planning to retire, she would know that I wanted her to. She was so stubborn that if she thought I wanted her to do something, there was no chance she would do it. But I felt confident that she was going to announce her retirement. So, I asked one of my superstars if she knew whether the librarian was going to take advantage of the early retirement incentive. After saying that she sure wished she would, the superstar volunteered to ask her inauspiciously. At the end of the day the superstar shared the bad news. The librarian was not going to retire! This was on a Tuesday and the deadline for accepting the early retirement incentive was the following Friday. There was little time to act. Remembering the philosophy of always treating difficult teachers as though they want to do what is right, I approached the difficult librarian with a plan.

On Wednesday, I sauntered into the library to have a nice chat with Mrs. Dewey. I expressed to Mrs. Dewey how orderly her library always was. She proudly shared her myriad rules, procedures, and fines structures that allowed her to maintain such order. (Plus they helped keep the students out!) I then shared with her that I was thinking about next year and how to utilize this excellent resource even more. I thought that it might be inspiring to the students to have a monthly theme in the library. Mrs. Dewey could put up signs in the media center advertising the theme and have displays supporting the theme. In addition, she could start a monthly newsletter developed around this concept. She could also highlight new materials and promote other resources to the students and staff. And, for her crowning glory, I would set aside 10 minutes at each monthly faculty meeting for her to promote the library, show or demonstrate new resources, and explain the monthly theme and why it was selected. We could also allow a few minutes each month for an "Ask the librarian" question-and-answer session. Since we met in the media center, it made sense to go ahead and take advantage of the opportunity to promote it.

Obviously, I knew that Mrs. Dewey was not fond of encouraging people to come into or use the library. I was also aware that she was not comfortable about the idea of speaking at the faculty meetings. Mrs. Dewey was not very fond of people or hard work. The next day, Mrs. Dewey turned in her retirement letter to me. A full day prior to the deadline.

I mentioned treating Mrs. Dewey as though she wanted to do what is right. As one can imagine, a good librarian would have loved the idea of a theme and newsletter. An effective librarian, when offered 10 minutes at each staff meeting to promote new materials, would have asked for 15. This approach allowed me to maintain communication with this difficult staff member and yet provided an incentive for her to take advantage of her retirement opportunity.

A temptation with difficult teachers is to reduce their impact by giving them smaller classes or less responsibility. It is tempting to limit their contact with students and parents. While this is not inherently a bad idea—minimizing harmful interactions with students is always recommended—do not make their jobs so easy that they will never want to retire. Developing a schedule or course load that minimizes the responsibilities of a difficult teacher may encourage the desire to continue working. When difficult staff members are eligible to retire, a principal might plan to increase their future workload. If you make things too easy, they will never quit.

Retirement is a wonderful way to eliminate some difficult teachers. The responsibility of the principal is to make sure they take advantage of this option when it is available. If a difficult staff member is eligible to retire in two years and there is no chance the staffer would quit before then, you may want to put time and energies into other endeavors. By the same token, you would want to make sure the teacher does not choose to stay three years.

## Building Transfers

I am not a believer in passing responsibilities to someone else. I also have no interest in inheriting another person's negative staff member. However, sometimes transfers can be effective. If a person has become too comfortable and too powerful, then a transfer may be an opportunity to start over. People might want to change, but they are not strong enough to stand up to peers. In situations such as this, teachers may benefit from a building transfer.

It is unfair to the students, staff, or principal to make any school a dumping ground for difficult staff members. Because a leader is effective is no reason to give this principal all problem teachers others cannot work with. That is just as unfair as giving your best teacher every challenging student in the school. Being judicious with this option is important in order to have the most effective school district possible. Taking difficult teachers out of the environment with which they are most familiar can dramatically increase their discomfort. It can also give them a clean slate, if they choose to take advantage of it. If these teachers are in the dismissal documentation process and they move schools, then they might enjoy an inappropriate reprieve.

In some circumstances transfers can be very effective. However, a great deal of thought is encouraged before moving difficult staff members.

## Discontinuing a Program

Although it may sound like something you would never consider, discontinuing a program may allow you to eliminate an extremely difficult staff member from your building. Addition by subtraction may be one way to look at it. If you have a strong negative influence who is a parent liaison, a Title teacher, or an at-risk teacher and this person is a drain on the school, discontinuation of their particular responsibilities may be an option. Be sensitive to which teacher may may be forced to leave the school. Some districts have policies requiring that employees with the least experience in the school be transferred if program eliminations jeopardize veteran faculty members.

Examine the pros and cons of losing any program if other approaches can successfully change this staff member's behavior. Consider whether there would be the possibility of reestablishing the programs with different personnel in the future.

# 20

# Dismissal

Dismissal of a difficult teacher should be a final alternative, because of the time involved. Some administrators feel that dismissing a tenured teacher is next to impossible. Administrators would prefer more direct ways to remove difficult teachers from our school. The bottom line, however, is that we cannot allow difficult teachers to continue to work with our students.

## Nonrenewal of Probationary Teachers

Let me make a distinction between dismissing a tenured teacher and denying contract renewal of a probationary staff member. Documenting in order to dismiss a tenured teacher may be long and arduous. Denying contract renewal of a probationary teacher is often more challenging emotionally than it is procedurally burdensome. This may be doubly true when other staff members like the non-tenured teacher. It can be compounded more when the principal considering the nonrenewal hired this staff member.

However, it is important to keep in mind the "opportunity cost" in allowing an ineffective probationary teacher to become tenured. This opportunity cost is paid in passing up the chance to hire an excellent teacher. One superstar or dynamic teacher leader can have a tremendous impact on an entire school. Keep in mind what settling for mediocrity can bring. Consider the diminished experiences that students must suffer if this ineffective teacher continues in education.

Remember that judiciously denying renewal to a teacher may *seem* like a tremendous emotional trauma for a school. Such may be the case during the process—and this feeling usually remains only for the rest of the school year. If an ineffective teacher leaves a school, this person leaves no significant legacy. Having a talented and energetic replacement at the start of the next year can erase most memories. If you do not make these difficult decisions now, the results may become overpowering in the future. Remember that the weakest employees are the least likely to leave on their own, because they lack other professional options.

## Dismissal of Tenured Teachers

Dismissals of tenured teachers primarily fall into three categories: incompetence, insubordination, and immorality. Different states may have various ways of defining grounds for the dismissal of tenured staff members, but in the majority of places these three areas form the predominant guidelines.

Although difficult teachers probably bring incompetence to mind, attempting to prove this should be your third option, if either of the others are possible. A tenured staff member *can* be dismissed for incompetence. And I would not dissuade any principal from pursuing this option. However, consider a number of factors before deciding to attempt to dismiss a teacher for incompetence. One is the amount of time and energy that can go into the documentation, remediation, and dismissal procedures. The content and tone of previous evaluations can thwart attempts to prove incompetence, whereas immorality and insubordination are less ambiguous. When you begin to evaluate and document with dismissal in mind, other options may become unavailable. Often the relationship between the principal and teacher become strained and this stress may affect other staff members. Stress increases with any type of dismissal, but because of the potentially lengthy process involved with an incompetency dismissal, heightened stress levels can adversely affect the whole school.

If you can show insubordination, this may be preferable to attempting to prove incompetence. Insubordination is more measurable and finite. Again, keep in mind your goal. If a teacher is incompetent, but you can dismiss him or her more quickly on grounds of insubordination, you should pursue insubordination.

I once worked with a teacher who was incompetent. This person had years of flowery evaluations from previous administrators. Dismissing this teacher for incompetence would not have created emotional upheaval in the school; it just would have been a very difficult and lengthy process. However, this teacher frequently left his class unsupervised. The teacher regularly made phone calls between classes, left school during planning time to run errands, or attended to personal business at lunch time. Running several minutes late because of errands, etc., the teacher left students unsupervised.

Although I had visited with this staff member about classroom performance and my concerns were documented in evaluations, I did not begin the remediation procedures for incompetence. I did not want the teacher on guard for limited short-term improvement. Instead I began documenting every tardiness and each time students were unsupervised. I wrote objectively: "Mr. Brown arrived at his classroom at 10:14. The bell to begin class rang at 10:09 and the students were left unsupervised by Mr. Brown until 10:14."

I would then ask Mr. Brown to sign the document, indicating that this matter had been discussed. I was not threatening in tone. I did not point my finger at his chest and say, "you had better not be late again or else." He was an adult who chose to perform unprofessionally. Interestingly, I seldom went out of my way to see whether he was late for class. He was so negligent and tardiness had developed into such a habit that he apparently had been doing this for years.

At the end of the first semester, I had documented over 20 instances of insubordination pertinent to class supervision. I successfully recommended his dismissal. If I had pursued incompetence—and believe me, he was—this process would have taken much more of my time and effort. Mr. Brown would have continued his negative impact on the students in the school for a much longer period of time.

In terms of showing evidence for dismissal, immorality is very similar to insubordination. Immoral acts are easily defined. The results of showing immorality are usually swift. A difficulty in pursuing dismissal on the basis of immorality is that often there is little time to make a decision. An event or behavior occurs and you are not prepared to make the dismissal decision. Often sympathy may influence you, if you have not prepared yourself to make difficult decisions. However, keeping in mind what is best for the students in your school can allow you to make the best decisions in all circumstances.

## Documentation—An Essential Element

Documenting inappropriate actions by staff members is critical in the effort toward dismissal. Although most school leaders have gone through principal training programs, few programs provide insight into the most effective methods of documentation for a teacher's dismissal. Do not be in a hurry to indicate you are attempting to dismiss a teacher. The later a teacher becomes aware of the potential for dismissal the easier it will be to accumulate documentation. The targeted staff member should always be aware of any document you may use toward dismissal. However, you do not need to threaten dismissal during the initial documentation gathering period.

The best way to document is to be factual and objective in your report. If you take this approach, there will be fewer opportunities for arguments and power struggles. When documenting classroom observations, record what is actually occurring. Avoid making opinionated commentary as you take notes. If a teacher is a poor classroom manager, documenting specific student behaviors at certain intervals is much more neutral and powerful than noting that the "students were out of control." Take notes that include specifics such as, "9:05, three students were out of their seats and pushing by the pencil sharpener; 9:11 two students had their heads down and appeared to be sleeping, one student was pulling the hair of another student; 9:17 teacher working at her desk, five students were . . . , etc." Facts are more difficult to refute. You should take notes such as this routinely during classroom visits. Later, when you share concerns about classroom management, you can have a more focused conversation and detailed written documentation of the problems that went on.

If the teacher offers explanations or excuses for why these students were behaving in this manner, feel free to add to the form after your conference: "As per conference: Mrs. X shared that this was a particularly bad day for her. She indicated that normally her classroom . . ." This validates any teacher, and would not detract from the witness the notes provide to dismissal proceedings.

Notes should be taken regarding unobserved behavior. If a parent calls and reports that a difficult teacher tore up his or her child's paper in front of the class or used obscene language, you can document the facts. Regardless of whether this behavior actually occurred, you can still write that "On March 6th at 2:25 a parent called and reported that Mr. James said . . ." Again, share this with the staff member. They teacher should sign the document acknowledging that he has read it. If a signature is refused, then add, "This information was shared with Mr. James on . . . and he refused to sign the document."

Please remember that I am talking about how to deal with difficult staff members. You do not necessarily need to document and have formal conferences with most teachers and events. As soon as you put pen to paper, you begin to lose some of the trust and diminish the relationship with the affected staff member. Use great discretion in the timing and use of formal documentation with any staff member.

My philosophy has always been this: "Raise the praise; minimize the criticize." Nevertheless, proceed with caution in using *written* praise with a teacher you may have to dismiss. Although the written praise may be specific, the written praise could work against you later. If you feel that praise might motivate them, praise verbally; it may be less likely to interfere with a future dismissal process.

Keep in mind during the process of non-renewal or dismissal, that there will be discomfort among the faculty in the school.

When I was working with the most disliked teacher in our school, the teachers' organization sent this staff member flowers during the process. Other faculty would tell this despised teacher to "hang in there!" Keeping your focus on what is best for kids will allow you to do what needs to be done. Be aware of the uneasiness that often comes with making difficult decisions, but do not allow it to prevent you from making the right decisions.

If you document effectively and confer with poor teachers in a professional and increasingly direct manner you may never reach the point of making a decision of nonrenewal or dismissal. When a teacher and support group are aware that you have an "airtight" case against them, the teacher will leave voluntarily. Remember your goal: the school will be a better place for the students.

# Part 8

# General Tips and Guidelines

# 21

# How Can I Stop Them from Sending so Many Students to the Office?

Many schools have one or two staff members who send 25 to 50 percent of all the students who are sent to the office for disciplinary reasons. In most cases, the students have committed minor infractions. Supporting these teachers is especially challenging, because their behavior is frequently as inappropriate as that of the student. If you discipline the student and have no further dialogue with the teacher, you have told the teacher that it is acceptable to send students to the office for minor offenses. You may even send the message that teachers are *supposed* to refer students for these offenses.

The time drain on the principal is damaging and costly. The larger proportion of hours and energy a school leader spends reacting, the less opportunity there will be to practice important proactive instructional leadership. If a principal can stop the

175

teacher from making inappropriate referrals, the leader is able to focus on effective leadership concerns.

If a teacher regularly sends students to the office for minor offenses without first contacting the parents, it becomes very difficult for the principal to support the teacher. Keep in mind that the majority of teachers who "nickel and dime" students regularly have poor relations with parents. This is because these teachers have angered so many parents over their teaching career. They have received angry notes and irate phone calls from parents. Their principals have spoken with them on many occasions regarding unhappy parents. These teachers are often afraid of contacting the parents of their students. If teachers do not initiate positive contact with parents, the majority of contact they have with parents will be negative. Require that the difficult teacher contact parents before sending students to the office. Tell the teachers who refer students for minor infractions that they may not send students to the office without first conferring with parents.

If a teacher sends a student to the office with a note that says, "This is the fifth time in the last two weeks Jimmy has come to class without a pencil" you would support this staff member initially. You may decide to punish this student, call a parent, and share the consequences. If you call the student's mother and share with her that her son is being given detention because he has come to class without a pencil five times, you are likely to get this reaction from his mom: "Why didn't I know?"

You might feel defensive because you realize that the mother is right. A rule of thumb I have for educational leaders is that they should never feel defensive. If they do, it may be because they or teachers are doing something wrong. In this case, the teacher was doing something inappropriate so you feel defensive when you attempt to support her.

Establishing expectations is essential in working with difficult staff members. Asking and expecting the staff to contact the parent *before* the student is sent to the office is an appropriate guideline. Realizing that some teachers may not regularly contact parents, providing them with some role modeling may be helpful. Explain that a call from the teacher is more effective because the teacher is asking for the parent's assistance—not establishing negative initial contact regarding a punishment. Offer teachers a "script" to work with: "Mrs. Johnson, I was wondering if I could get your help on something. Jimmy has forgotten a pencil three times in the last week. I was not sure if you were aware of this, but I wanted to request your assistance before he ends up falling behind in class or before the office has to get involved. Could I get your help in visiting with him and making sure that he leaves for school prepared? Your assistance would greatly be appreciated."

Few parents would not agree to help. If the first contact is made in the form of a request for assistance, the teacher can build a positive relationship with a parent. A few parents will not follow through and at some point the office may be involved. However the difference is that the principal will not feel defensive because the parent "did not know"; the parent will feel on the spot because she did not follow through on her word. The point is not to make the parent feel defensive, but to make sure the educators are not back pedaling. Once this expectation is established, the teachers who make this initial contact will prevent many office referrals.

It is probably also safe to assume that merely asking and expecting the faculty to make preventive parental contact will not cause them to stop the parade of students to the office. You can use their resistance to contact parents to your advantage. When this teacher continues in the pattern of frequent referrals for minor issues, you can intervene. You can start by treating them as though they are doing what is right. Ask the difficult teacher what the parent said when called. Again, expect that the difficult teacher always wants to do what is correct. The teacher will probably offer an excuse about not having time to call. After hearing repeated excuses regarding no parent contact, try this.

On the next occasion that this teacher sends a student to the office for something about which the teacher should have contacted the parent, put a note in the teacher's mailbox asking him or her to stop by your office during their conference period. Have the phone number of the parent handy. When the teacher stops by the office offer a chair.

Then, again expecting the teacher to do what is right, ask what the parent said when called about this patterned behavior. Assuming the difficult teacher will make up an excuse for not calling, calmly say, "Oh, well, I have the phone number right here." Then dial the phone number and hand the teacher the receiver. Treat the teacher as though he or she wants to do what is right.

Assuming that the teacher has a high level of concern about contacting parents, the teacher will refrain from referring students for minor offenses. Although *never* do this with an effective staff member, it is fine for the difficult teacher to leave your office and tell the other teachers what happened. As a matter of fact, if the teacher tells enough people, other difficult staff might choose to reduce the stream of students they send to the office simply out of their own fear of parents.

# 22

# If All Else Fails— General Tips, Guidelines, and Reminders

Deciding when to first approach a difficult staff member is a challenge. Your first contacts and efforts toward improving a challenging teacher are important in continuing to develop a relationship between principal and teacher. A rule to keep in mind is this: "If a teacher realizes that you are aware of an inappropriate behavior, you must have a dialogue regarding the behavior."

## If They Know You Are Aware of It, They Know You Accept It

If you become aware that a teacher is using an approach that you feel is unacceptable, deciding when and how to approach that person is difficult. Take some time to decide on a strategy so that you may approach the teacher professionally and effectively. You might decide to wait until it occurs again, put it off indefinitely, or talk about it at your discretion. However, this flexibility evaporates once the teacher knows you are aware of the behavior.

If you become the new principal of a school you might establish the expectation that at the school adults do not "yell" at students. Perhaps, during the second week of school you are in the hallway and a teacher loses his or her cool and starts yelling in class. If no one knows you heard this, you may not want to visit with that teacher for a variety of reasons. One might be that you do not want your first contact with a staff member to be seen as negative. Another may be that you hope that this is the only time all year the teacher will do this and you may not need to address it. You may also be so busy that you feel that this is not your highest priority. Let it pass. Any of the reasons may be very valid and justifiable.

The dynamic becomes different, however, if the teacher learns that you heard the yelling. I feel that once teachers become aware you know of inappropriate approaches it is important to touch base with them. You may gently ask whether everything is okay because you heard yelling. I very much believe that approaching matters informally works best.

It is important not to validate behavior by ignoring it. The importance of some type of acknowledgment is that what you accept becomes the standard. It becomes much more difficult and emotional to begin to address a behavior months after it first occurred. The awkwardness and emotional baggage that can develop in both parties can increase the potential volatility as you work to improve the situation. Validating inappropriate behavior can become particularly troubling, if it results in a great number of disciplinary referrals.

## Never Argue or Raise Your Voice with a Difficult Teacher

A principal should avoid getting in an argument with any staff member, especially a difficult teacher. This does not mean to avoid disagreements. I am talking about arguing or yelling. Arguing belligerently is unprofessional and offers poor role modeling. This is the same standard a principal should have in working with students. You should never argue with or yell at any students. Remember, difficult teachers are probably better at arguing than you are. They have practiced argumentation and they are most comfortable when interacting this way. Do not climb into the boxing rings into which difficult teachers invite you. Stay outside the ring and make them feel uncomfortable.

## Hope They Run Out and Tell Their Peers

If you consistently work with difficult teachers in a professional manner, then you have no reason to be concerned with what these staff members tell their peers. In Chapter 21 I share a method to help reduce the number of students your poorest staff members refer to the office for discipline. The concluding point is, if you effectively work with one challenging staff member, and what you did with them is shared with other ineffective teachers, there may be no need for you to work with the other teachers. As a matter of fact, if they tell other difficult teachers, then you may only have to use this approach one time to affect the two or three teachers who continually refer students.

This "word of mouth" information may be disconcerting enough to alter the behavior of their negative peers.

I had a teacher who resigned after almost 30 years of service. This teacher quit because he was going to have to observe three other teachers as part of his remediation process. One of the teachers he was expected to observe was a longtime peer at another school who, unlike himself, was very effective. Another teacher my difficult staff member was supposed to visit was a first-year staff member with only three months' experience. This difficult teacher was so embarrassed, he resigned the next day. When he resigned, he brought in copies of the expectations that I had developed for him, made copies, and laid them around the teachers' workroom. When someone told me what he did, he could not believe that I was not upset by this. I was glad that he shared the expectations for someone who is harming students. Teachers should be aware of possible outcomes of refusing to make any attempts to improve their teaching performance. I had treated him as though the entire staff were watching. Thus, there was nothing negative about him telling others. It probably made my job easier. The numerous positive staff members saw the expectations as reasonable and proper. The few remaining difficult teachers had an increased level of concern as a result.

If you handle things professionally, you are unlikely to achieve negative results; you can actually have a far-reaching positive influence with other challenging faculty.

## Use a Shotgun Approach

When dealing with difficult teachers, remember that each is different. Although I have presented many suggestions in the preceding pages, there is no panacea. Use a shotgun approach with difficult teachers. Feel free to use a combination of approaches simultaneously. Make them uncomfortable, reduce their influence on other staff, continually attempt to motivate them, always be aware of opportunities to eliminate them, etc. Come at these challenging negative faculty from any combination of directions. You may never know what will be effective or when it might work.

Avoid the temptation to *tell* them what to do. Telling anyone what to do is seldom, if ever, effective. Invoking directives should be used selectively. Belligerent people resist any directives, though not always overtly. Telling them what to do also gives them a cause to fight and focus. Using a shotgun approach involving a variety of methods will prevent them from organizing an effective defense.

# 23

# Easing the Guilt

The difficult teachers in your school have long been thorns in the sides of your positive staff. The productive and effective teachers in your school have grown tired of the power these negative staff yield. They are tired of avoiding the teachers' workroom because of a few people and the environment they cultivate. The positive innovators have become weary of these few teachers who fight every positive program. Most importantly, the effective, caring professionals are sickened by the way the students they value are treated every day when they walk into these ineffective teachers' classrooms. They do not want *any* student in the school to be dehumanized or belittled.

During a documentation, remediation, and dismissal process, the teachers may have a kind word for their ineffective peers. They may tell them to "hang in there" or that they are thinking of them. They may even be a part of a teachers' group that sends flowers. But, trust me, they will not send them any more flowers once they are finally gone from the school. The only person who wants the kids in your school to be treated in the manner they deserve more than your best staff members is you.

## Should You Feel Guilty?

There is not one thing in this book that is easy. There is not one suggestion in this book that is fun for the principal. Dealing with difficult teachers is never enjoyable. It may be the least plea-surable thing a principal does. We are all caring people. Having empathy for others is probably one of the reasons we chose edu-cation. There is no doubt that the great concern we have for oth-ers is one of the reasons we have chosen to devote our lives to education. Thus, any principal who has ever attempted to lace up the work boots and deal effectively with a difficult staff mem-ber has probably struggled with this question: "Is what I am doing the right thing?" Guilt is probably an emotion that has entered your hearts and conscience. It was something I struggled with tremendously. I know that teaching is the most important profession there is. I have greater respect for educators than I do any other professionals. Some of these difficult people have been teaching for years. Many of them have families who rely on them.

So, I have struggled many times with the question, "Should I feel guilty?"

Finally, I came to the realization that as a principal your goal has to be to do what is best for the students. I realized that you should not ever feel guilty about doing what is best for the young people in your buildings. You should only feel guilty, if you do not.

# References

Behling, H. E. (1984). *The effective school*. Information Analyses. (ERIC Document Reproduction Service No. ED 257 222).

Bissell, B. (1992, July. The paradoxical leader. Paper presented at the Missouri Leadership Academy, Columbia, MO.

Burr, A. (1993, September). *Being an effective principal*. Paper presented at the regional satellite meeting of the Missouri Leadership Academy, Columbia, MO.

Covey, S. R. (1989). *The 7 habits of highly effective people*. New York: Simon & Schuster.

Danley, W. L., & Burch, B. G. (1978). Teacher perceptions of the effective instructional leader. *The Clearing House, 52*, 78–79.

Edmonds, R. (1981). *Improving the effectiveness of New York City public schools*. (ERIC Document Reproduction Service No. ED 243 980).

Fiore, D. (1999). The relationship between principal effectiveness and school culture in elementary schools. (Doctoral dissertation, Indiana State University, Terre Haute, 1999).

Foriska, T. J. (1994). The principal as instructional leader: Teaming with teachers for student success. *Schools in the Middle, 3*(3), 31–34.

Gardner, H. (1993). *Frames of mind: the theory of multiple intelligences*. New York: BasicBooks.

Garten, T. & Valentine, J. (1989). Strategies for faculty involvement in effective schools. *NASSP Bulletin, 73*(515), 1–7.

Glatthorn, A. (1984). *Differentiated supervision*. Alexandria, VA: Association for Supervision and Curriculum Development.

Harris, S. (1997). Five guidelines for a successful site-based administrator to follow. *NASSP Bulletin, 81* (588) 76–80.

Keefe, J. W., Clark, D. C., Nickerson, N. C., & Valentine, J. (1983). *The middle level principalship: The effective middle level principal, Volume II*. Reston, VA: National Association of Secondary School Principals.

Keefe, J., Kelley, E., & Miller, S. (1985). School climate: clear definitions and a model for a larger setting. *NASSP Bulletin, 69*(484), 70–77.

Lashway, L. (1988). Instruments for evaluation. *The School Administrator, 55* (9), 14–18.

McEwan, E. K. (1994). *Seven steps to effective instructional leadership*. New York: Scholastic, Inc.

Lipham, J. (1981). *Effective principal, effective school*. Reston, VA: National Association of Secondary Schools.

McEwan, E. K. (1994). *Seven steps to effective instructional leadership*. New York: Scholastic, Inc.

Podesta, C. (Speaker). (1996). *Life would be easy . . .if it weren't for change*. (Cassette Recording No. AASA96-314). Reston, VA: American Association of School Administrators.

Podesta, C. (Speaker). (1994). *Life Would Be Easy If It Weren't For Other People*. (Videocassette Recording). Plano, TX: Connie Podesta.

Purkey, C. S., & Smith, M. S. (1982). Too soon to cheer? Synthesis of research on effective schools. *Educational Leadership, 49,* 64–69.

Roeschlein, T. (2002). What effective middle school principals do to impact school climate. (Doctoral dissertation, Indiana State University, Terre Haute, 2002).

Rutherford, W. L. (1985). School principals as effective leaders. *Phi Delta Kappan, 67*(1), 31–34.

Schlechty, P. C. (1993). On the frontier of school reform with trailblazers, pioneers, and settlers. *Journal of Staff Development, 14*(4), 46–51.

Snyder, K. J., Krieger, R., & McCormick, R. (1983). School improvement goal setting: a collaborative model. *NASSP Bulletin, 67*(465), 60–65.

Stronge, J. H. (1993). Defining the principalship: instructional leader or middle manager. *NASSP Bulletin*, 77(553), 1–7.

Turner, E. (2002). What effective principals do to improve instruction and increase student achievement. (Doctoral dissertation, Indiana State University, Terre Haute, 2002).

Vroom, V. H. & Jago, A. G. (1988). *The new leadership: managing participation in organizations*. Englewood Cliffs, NJ: Prentice-Hall.

Walker, J. E. (1990). The skills of exemplary principals. *NASSP Bulletin*, 74(524), 48–55.

Webster, W. G., Sr. (1994). *Learner-centered principalship: The Principal as teacher of teachers*. Westport, CT: Praeger Publishers.

Whitaker, M. E. (1997). Principal leadership behaviors in school operations and change implementations in elementary schools in relation to climate. (Doctoral dissertation, Indiana State University, Terre Haute, 1997).

Whitaker, T. (1997). Three differences between "more effective" and "less effective" middle level principals. *Current Issues In Middle Level Education*, 6(2), 54–64.

Whitaker, T. (1998). Principal priorities. Unpublished manuscript, Indiana State University, Terre Haute.

Whitaker, T. & Lumpa, D. (1995). "Hi, I'm the new principal": making your first year work. *Schools In The Middle*, 5(2), 41–43.

Whitaker, T., Whitaker, B., and Lumpa, D. (2000). *Motivating and inspiring teachers: The educational leader's guide for building staff morale*. Larchmont, NY: Eye on Education.

If you'd like information about
inviting Todd Whitaker to speak to your group,
please contact him at **t-whitaker@indstate.edu** or
his web site **www.toddwhitaker.com** or (812)237-2904.